GARDENING FROM SEED

GARDENING FROM SEED

THE KEYS TO SUCCESS WITH
FLOWERS AND VEGETABLES

A MARTHA STEWART LIVING BOOK

Distributed simultaneously by
Clarkson N. Potter, Inc., Leisure Arts, and
Martha Stewart Living Omnimedia

Manufactured in the United States of America.

Text by Thomas Christopher
Editors: Margaret Roach and
Douglas Brenner
Art Director: Ivette Montes de Oca
Gardening Editors:
Andrew Beckman and James A. Bielaczyc
Assistant Art Director: Sharon Slaughter
Copy Editor: Talley Sue Hohlfeld

CREDITS

PHOTOGRAPHY Christopher Baker, pages 16, 75 (center left and bottom);
Reed Davis, pages 22 (right), 28 (left); Richard Felber, pages 13, 14, 24-25, 35, 91
(bottom); Gentl & Hyers, page 79 (top left and right); Lisa Hubbard, pages 2, 7 (bottom right), 30 (all except far left center), 38, 48, 60-63 (bottom), 64-74 (top and center
right), 76 (center right and bottom), 77 (all except center right), 79 (bottom), 80
(top), 81 (bottom), 82, 83 (bottom), 84-87, 88-90, 92-111; Thibault Jeanson, page 91
(top); Kit Latham, page 55; Elliston Lutz, cover, pages 1, 6, 7 (top left), 8-9, 20, 29
(bottom left and right), 33, 45 (far left); James Merrell, page 39; Matthew Septimus,
pages 7 (top right), 27, 28 (right), 29 (top left and right), 32, 43, 44, 45 (center and
right); United States Department of Agriculture, Agricultural Research Service, page
47; Jonelle Weaver, page 22 (left); Anna Williams, pages 3, 30 (far left center), 63
(top), 74 (bottom), 76 (top), 77 (center right), 78, 80 (bottom), 81 (top), 83 (top)
ILLUSTRATION Linda Heppes Funk, pages 52-53, 56, 58; Kevin Sprouls, page 19

Library of Congress Cataloging in
Publication Data is available upon request.
ISBN 0–609-80665-3

ACKNOWLEDGMENTS

PLANTING THE SEEDS FOR THIS BOOK required the time, energy, and dedication of a great many people. Special thanks to Thomas Christopher, whose passion for gardening is evident on every page. Thank you, too, to the art directors, editors, art production staff and others whose ideas and efforts contributed to the creation of this volume, notably Akiko Carver, Gabrielle Chasin-Simon, Jonathan Chernes, Ava Chin, Stephanie Garcia, Kathleen Hackett, Jennifer Hitchcox, Nicole Lobisco, Melissa Morgan, George Planding, Tracey Reavis, Nikki Rooker, Curtis Smith, Gael Towey, Sarah Trigg, and Alison Vanek; and to everyone at W. Atlee Burpee & Co., Satellite Graphics, and Quebecor Printing. Finally, thank you to Martha, for inspiring us to reach for the best.

CONTENTS

PART

PART

PART

INTRODUCTION

A SEED

IS A MAGICAL THING. A FAT, PALE BEAN, a flint-hard corn kernel, the chafflike seed of a marigold, or a speck from a coleus blossom—in the most important way these, and every other seed, are alike. Within their tiny, inert bodies, all of them hide an endless potential. Take any healthy seed, satisfy its simple requirements, and it will swell, split, shoot upward, and unfurl, as from it emerges a whole new life.

No matter how many times I watch this process happen, it always feels brand new. The germination of spring's first seed is the most exciting moment of the gardening year. As that delicate green finger pops up through the surface of the soil, I feel again the same thrill I felt as a young girl, watching the very first seedling emerge from a cut-off milk carton my father and I had carefully filled with dirt, planted with mail-order seeds, and set out in our sunny kitchen.

DESIGNED TO GROW

These days, I meet all too many grown-up gardeners who say they can't be bothered with starting from seed. They're convinced that the process is complicated and demanding—that too many things can go wrong. But they're ignoring an essential fact of life that I learned from my father: Nature designed seeds to grow. Raising seedlings is a process at which anyone can succeed by applying a few easily learned skills. These are laid out in the following pages, along with the tricks that professionals and experienced home gardeners use to get the best results.

For success with seeds, you also need the right equipment. Luckily, though, everything you'll require is simple, inexpensive, and easy to obtain. Check with that neighbor who claims starting from seed is too much trouble, and you'll probably find he just stuck seeds into dirt and then trusted to the weather or placed his pots on a drafty windowsill. He guaranteed his own failure. You, on the other hand, have this book to help you find all the necessary tools, and to give you advice on making them work with the seeds you choose.

NEW CHOICES, TIMELESS REWARDS

There are many practical advantages to starting plants from seed. To begin with, it saves money. Become your own nurseryman, and you can raise a whole gardenful of flowers and vegetables for the same price you'd pay for a few six-packs of nursery transplants. More important, starting from seed opens up new worlds of gardening opportunities.

If you want to grow annual flowers, for example, and you rely on local nurseries to start plants for you, you'll have your choice of maybe two dozen different varieties: one or two brash marigolds, a couple of petunias, a red-flowered geranium and a white-flowered one, some packs of impatiens and coleus in mixed colors, pansies, wax begonias, and precious little else. But if you are willing to start the plants at home, you'll find thousands of different varieties at your disposal, including the latest introductions, "new" to the trade that season. The selection encompasses flowers in every imaginable color, size, and shape, such as white marigolds and chartreuse zinnias, cosmos with fluted petals, and dwarf salvias. There's a plant for every niche in your garden, whether it's shady or sunny, wet or dry.

Starting from seed is also your entrée into the intriguing world of heirloom plants. You can't really reproduce the rich flavor of your grandmother's sun-dried tomatoes, say, unless you start with the same fruits she did, the 'Principe Borghese' tomatoes whose seeds she brought from Italy. You won't find them as off-the-shelf seedlings at the garden center. You'll have to do as Grandmother did and start those heirlooms from seed.

Equally rewarding varieties of almost every flower, herb, and vegetable are yours to discover—and along the way, you may even tickle the interest of a son or daughter, or a grandchild. Children are quick to grasp the magic that is in a seed. Plant one together, and you'll be giving them an experience they can enjoy, year after year, for the rest of their lives. At Turkey Hill, my home in Connecticut, I'm constantly experimenting with flowers and vegetables that are new to me, but I always leave room for a few of the same hybrid columbines and 'Big Boy' tomatoes that my father proudly grew from seed in his yard in New Jersey.

HOW TO USE THIS BOOK

With the help of our garden experts at *Martha Stewart Living,* I've organized this book the same way nature has organized the gardening year. Part One begins indoors, with tips on shopping for seeds and everything you need to know—and do—to start seedlings for warm-weather plants such as tomatoes, basil, and zinnias, which need to get a jump on the growing season. The rest of the chapter explains this process step-by-step, right through easing a seedling's transition from its cozy indoor "nursery" to a life amid the elements outdoors.

By the time the last frosts are passing and the soil has thawed, every gardener is impatient to be outdoors. Part Two focuses on the seed sowing you can do in the garden, employing the same techniques for planting directly into flower beds and vegetable patches that have proven successful at Turkey Hill as well as in other gardens in every region of the country. We've given you handy checklists that specify the ideal moment for putting in each type of seed, tips on getting seeds off to a solid start, and a guide to summer and fall sowings that can produce a second harvest of flowers and edible crops.

Part Three supplies practical plans for both a cutting garden and a kitchen garden, and finally, the Plant Glossary. An encyclopedia in brief, the glossary has concise entries on more than one hundred kinds of seeds, arranged in alphabetical order. You'll find all you need to know to grow each kind of seed, together with essential facts about the plant and its use in the garden. Success at seed starting isn't just growing healthy plants—it's growing exactly the plants you want and need.

Martha Stewart

MARTHA STEWART

STARTING SEEDS
INDOORS

PART 1

Why Bother?

It might seem simpler, and easier, just to plant your seeds directly into the garden where they are to grow, rather than sowing them into pots indoors. Of course, it *is* easier to plant seeds right into the ground (this is called direct sowing). But it doesn't always work. Many of the flowers and vegetables we've come to regard as fixtures are actually exotic visitors from other regions with distinctly different climates. Peppers, tomatoes, and petunias, for example, originated in warmer

climates, and their seeds won't germinate in the chilly soil of the spring most North Americans experience. If we wait until the soil has warmed before we sow these plants, the seeds will germinate, but there will not be enough warm days left in the growing season for the resulting plants to bear flowers and fruit before an autumn frost cuts them down. To give these plants the prolonged stretch of warm weather they require to mature, we have to sow their seeds indoors.

Other plants, by contrast, need a head start because they hate heat. Many annual flowers—snapdragons and sweet peas, for instance—originated in areas with prolonged periods of cool, moist weather, such as occur during Mediterranean winters and springs. In most regions of the United States, spring slips from frigid to hot so quickly that cool-season annuals don't have time to mature and flower—unless we extend their spring by starting them indoors. In the Deep South, where summer is the season of most extreme weather, gardeners save many cool-loving flowers and vegetables for fall planting. To give these plants a head start, Southerners must sow the seeds in summertime, beginning indoors where it's cooler because the seeds would bake if sowed outside in hot, dry soil.

COPING WITH DAY LENGTH

Other plants, such as the annual flower bachelor's button and some onions, often require an earlier start than outdoor sowing can give them because their blossoming or bulb-making is triggered by changes in day length. What if, like Martha, you garden in a northern climate and want to grow some special onion—a 'Benny's Red,' say, which isn't to be found among the limited variety of onion sets (little bulblets) most nurseries sell in the spring? You'll have to buy that onion as seed, and you must start the seeds indoors in January or February if you want a crop. This will ensure that your plants will have matured before the arrival of summer's short nights makes them switch to bulb production. That reaction is genetically programmed; those plants are going to make bulbs then whether they're ready or not. Wait until spring to sow onion seeds outdoors, and summer nights will force the still-infant plants to stop growing and instead make onion bulbs so tiny they're useable only in martinis.

EXTENDING THE HARVEST

Starting seeds indoors not only increases the variety of vegetables available to the gardener, it can also extend the harvest season. By all means, wait until your soil has thawed and drained, and then plant lettuce seeds right into the moist soil of the garden. But at the same time, transplant into the same bed a couple dozen seedlings you started indoors, three or four weeks earlier. You will be able to eat salads harvested from the transplants while you wait for the seeds you just sowed to grow into plants.

CONTROLLING THE ENVIRONMENT

A prime reason for starting seeds indoors is that *you* control the environment there. If you are growing seeds that demand certain conditions, such as tomatoes and petunias, which require extra heat, it's best to sow them indoors where you can ensure that they get what they need. Likewise, because you can provide ideal conditions indoors, you'll find that the rate of germination—the percentage of the seeds that sprout and grow—is far higher.

Finally, there are no natural disasters indoors: no crows to devour the seeds, no floods to wash them away, no cutworms to fell the seedlings, and no freak late frosts to nip the tender foliage. When sowing seeds that are precious or rare, why entrust them to fickle weather and hungry wildlife?

SHOPPING FOR SEEDS

All seeds are not equal. The success of any sowing depends on the quality of the seed you start with. Freshness is critical. The viability of seeds—the reliability of their germination—dwindles with age. Even the best-quality seed may not be very good if it has been sitting on a shelf for a year or two.

This potential varies from species to species.

Onion and parsley seeds, for example, lose their viability quickly, within a year or so of being packaged, whereas cucumber and spinach seeds may stay viable for five years or more if they are properly stored. To be safe, though, purchase only seeds packed for the present growing season. The year for which seeds were packed should be printed clearly on the packet.

For the same reasons, be careful of where you buy seeds. The neighborhood hardware store may offer bargain prices, but chances are its seeds have not been stored in a climate-controlled room. Expose packaged seeds to repeated temperature swings and high humidity, and again their viability drops. Your best assurance of good quality is to buy seeds from a supplier you know and trust.

EVALUATING PROCESSED SEEDS

When shopping for seeds, you are likely to come across the following terms:

PELLETED SEED Minuscule seeds are sometimes coated with a biodegradable material that adds bulk, transforming them into pellets, which are easier to handle. Keep in mind, however, that pelleted seeds almost always cost more than unpelleted ones, and that their coating may include fungicides.

SEED TAPE The seeds have been imbedded in a water-soluble tape and spaced at the proper interval for planting outdoors. Just stretch the tape out on prepared soil, bury the tape to the indicated depth, and your sowing is done. Seed tape is more expensive than loose seed, but it is also more convenient for very young gardeners and for older gardeners with arthritic fingers.

COATED, OR TREATED, SEEDS Some types of seed, notably sweet corn, that are especially vulnerable to fungi, may have been coated with fungicides before they were packed. Organic gardeners, beware!

WORDS TO KNOW

THERE'S A MINE OF USEFUL INFORMATION PRINTED ON MOST SEED PACKETS. IN ADDITION TO GIVING INSTRUCTIONS FOR GROWING THE PLANT, THE PACKET WILL HELP YOU DECIDE WHETHER OR NOT A PARTICULAR VARIETY SUITS YOUR NEEDS AND WHETHER YOU WANT TO GROW THAT PLANT AT ALL. THE PROBLEM IS, MUCH OF THIS INFORMATION IS WRITTEN IN A KIND OF HORTICULTURAL SHORTHAND. THE FOLLOWING GLOSSARY WILL ENABLE YOU TO DECIPHER ANY PACKET.

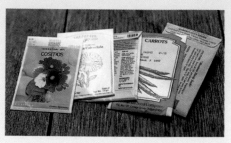

ANNUAL
A plant that completes its life cycle—starting from seed, maturing, flowering, and bearing seed or fruit—in a single growing season. Because an annual commonly dies at the end of the growing season, if you want the same plant next year, you will have to replant (unless it self-sows; see Self-Sow, facing page).

BIENNIAL
A plant that ordinarily requires two growing seasons to complete its life cycle. Traditionally, most biennials were sown into the garden in late summer or early fall, so that the resulting plants could bloom the following spring or summer. But if started indoors in late winter or very early spring, many biennials will bloom in the garden during their first season of growth.

BOTTOM HEAT
Warmth provided by electric heating cables or mats to promote the germination of seeds started indoors. For a fuller explanation and an easier alternative, see The Right Light, page 19.

DAMPING OFF
A disease caused by a number of soil-borne fungi. After germination, infected seedlings grow but then suddenly topple over at soil level, and die. To discourage damping off, always use a sterile seed-starting mix. For more on damping off, see pages 26, 28, and 32.

DAYS TO HARVEST
Regularly included on vegetable seed packets, this specifies the number of days, on average, that the plant requires to grow from sowing to a state in which the crop is ready to be harvested.

DOUBLE
A term that describes a flower with more petals than is typical for that species. Most florist's chrysanthemums, for example, are double. A hybrid tea rose is double, too, in contrast to a five-petaled wild rose, which is single; see Single, facing page.

GROW ON
To give a specific kind of care to a seedling after germination and before transplanting into the garden. "Grow on cool," for instance, means that you should keep the seedlings cool, typically at fifty to sixty degrees.

HARDEN OFF
To ready seedlings for the transition from their indoor growing area to their home in the garden. For a fuller explanation of this procedure, see Hardening Off, page 32.

HARDY
Describes a plant adapted to survive the local climate without artificial protection; most often used to indicate tolerance for winter cold. Hardiness is commonly expressed in terms of the United States Department of Agriculture Zones of Hardiness Map (see page 47).

HEIRLOOM { An antique flower or vegetable variety, commonly a regional or ethnic favorite ignored by mass-market seed companies. Most heirlooms are valued for their distinctive flavor, hardiness, or old-fashioned charm. Usually, seeds collected from these plants produce seedlings with the same characteristics as the parents, and so once purchased, an heirloom can be preserved from year to year.

HYBRID { A plant produced by mating (crossing) two distinctly different varieties or species.

F1 HYBRID The first generation of seed produced by crossing. As a rule, F1 hybrid seed produces plants more vigorous than either parent. The seed also develops into plants with uniform characteristics.

F2 HYBRID A second-generation hybrid, raised from seed harvested from an F1 hybrid. F2 hybrids lack the vigor and uniformity of their F1 parents.

LAST FROST DATE { A common guide for calculating when to start seeds. Seed packets often recommend starting a certain number of weeks before the "last frost date." Based on local meteorological records, this is the average date in the spring when air temperatures may be expected to remain above thirty-two degrees in a given area. When planting seeds for late crops , you may encounter references to the "first frost date," the average date in the fall when temperatures first drop to thirty-two degrees or below. To learn the last and first frost dates in your area, check with your public library or call the local Cooperative Extension office (see the county or state listing in your phone book).

Because the last frost date is an average date, there is always some danger of frost in the days immediately following it. For this reason, the instructions on Martha's seed packets and in the Plant Glossary (see page 60) often recommend waiting to plant out particularly cold-sensitive species until "all danger of frost is past." To ascertain that date, consult nurseries or experienced gardeners in your area.

PERENNIAL { A plant that can persist from year to year, flowering and bearing seed each growing season. In the North, many perennials die back to the ground in the fall, with new growth sprouting from the roots in the spring.

SCARIFY { To pierce a seed's hard, waterproof coat. Seeds with such coverings must by scarified before they can germinate; see Before You Sow, page 26, for a description of this process.

SEED COAT { The outermost, protective layer of a seed; see Scarify, above.

SELF-SOW { To sow seed as part of a plant's life cycle, without human intervention. Some plants, if the flowers are not snipped off as they age and wilt, will drop seeds onto the soil. These self-sown seeds may give rise to "volunteer" seedlings the next year. These can be welcome, as in the case of cleome and bachelor's button (see Desirable Self-Sowers, page 18). If too prolific, however, volunteers may become weeds.

SINGLE { A flower with a single ring of petals; see Double, facing page.

TRUE LEAVES { A seedling's first leaf or pair of leaves to appear. Upon germination, a seedling may emerge as a simple shoot or bear one or two cotyledons (also called seed leaves), which are actually part of the seed embryo. The true leaves appear after the cotyledons.

FROM SEED TO SEEDLING

A SEED, WHETHER SOWN indoors or out, has four basic needs that must be met.

MOISTURE: A dormant seed may contain as little as two percent water by weight. Because this water content may need to increase to eighty percent before the embryo inside the seed will start growing, it is vital that newly sown seeds get enough water. At the same time, though, a seed can drown if kept continuously wet. Sowing into a good seed-starting mix is the best way to ensure that seeds get proper moisture. The mix should absorb water readily, but also allow excess to drain.

OXYGEN: A light, fluffy seed-starting mix will contain enough air to supply adequate oxygen for seed growth. Overwatering, however, by filling the pores in the mix, drives out the air and "stifles" your seeds.

WARMTH: A steady temperature of seventy to seventy-five degrees enhances the germination of most kinds of seeds, increasing the percentage that grow while also quickening the rate at which they sprout. Setting containers of starting mix and seeds on an electrically powered horticultural heating cable will maintain the ideal temperature. But you can achieve the same effect with less expense by using the simple seed-starting system outlined on the facing page.

LIGHT VS. DARK: Some seeds won't germinate until they are exposed to light; others germinate most readily in darkness. You'll find the right prescription for almost any seed in the Plant Glossary (page 60).

DESIRABLE SELF-SOWERS

IF THEY FIND YOUR CLIMATE, SOIL, AND SITE HOSPITABLE, MANY ANNUAL AND PERENNIAL FLOWERS TEND TO SELF-SOW IN THE GARDEN. SOME TOO-AGGRESSIVE SPECIES MAY BECOME PROBLEMS BY CROWDING OUT OTHER DESIRABLE PLANTS. BUT ESTABLISHING A SELF-SUSTAINING COLONY OF THE FOLLOWING PLANTS CAN KEEP A GARDEN BEAUTIFUL, WITH NO REPLANTING BY THE GARDENER (YOU SHOULD, HOWEVER, THIN SEEDLINGS ONCE THEY'RE ESTABLISHED). WHEN CHOOSING WHICH VOLUNTEERS TO LEAVE IN PLACE, FAVOR THE MOST VIGOROUS SEEDLINGS. THESE PLANTS' EXTRA STRENGTH MAY INDICATE THAT A PARTICULARLY HARDY, HEALTHY STRAIN IS DEVELOPING IN YOUR GARDEN, OR IT MAY JUST MARK THOSE PLANTS THAT HAVE FOUND A PARTICULARLY SUITABLE NICHE. WHATEVER THE CASE, A HEALTHIER PLANT IS FAR MORE LIKELY TO PROVE TROUBLE FREE.

BACHELOR'S BUTTON
(Centaurea cyanus)

CLEOME
(Cleome hassleriana)

COSMOS
(Cosmos spp.)

DILL
(Anethum graveolens)

DRUMMOND PHLOX
(Phlox drummondii)
Most likely to self-sow on sandy soils

GLOBE AMARANTH
(Gomphrena globosa)
A reliable self-sower in the Southeast

HOLLYHOCK
(Alcea rosea)
Single-flowered types often self-sow

JOHNNY-JUMP-UP
(Viola tricolor)
Commonly colonizes lawns

LARKSPUR
(Consolida ambigua)

MARIGOLD
(Tagetes spp.)
More compact French marigolds are most likely to volunteer

PETUNIA
(Petunia x hybrida)
Offspring bear small flowers

in a wide range of pink, purple, and white shades

POPPY
(Papaver somniferum)

ROSE MOSS, SUN PLANT, OR ELEVEN O'CLOCK
(Portulaca grandiflora)

SWEET ALYSSUM
(Lobularia maritima)

VERBENA BONARIENSIS
(Verbena bonariensis)
Tall, up to six feet

ZINNIA
(Zinnia elegans)

SEEDS AND SEEDLINGS are connoisseurs of light. To flourish, they demand specific minimum intensities of light, beaming specific mixes of colors, for specific numbers of hours every day. It's easy to meet these needs by building the system shown here, using items sold at any home center or hardware store.

But wouldn't it be simpler to set seed pots and trays on a sunny windowsill? The fact is, very few windowsills receive enough light to keep seedlings strong. Even a south-facing window admits only a small fraction of the rays. And in late winter, when you'll be starting most seeds, the sun is low in the sky and its light is weak.

You'll get far better results by germinating seeds and growing seedlings under a fluorescent-light system. As a bonus, the lights also warm the mix in seed-starting containers to a temperature perfect for germination.

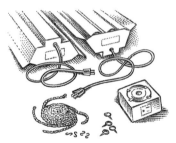

STEP ONE: You'll need a pair of two-tube, 4-foot-long fluorescent light fixtures; no-frills models sold as "shop lites" are inexpensive and reliable. For the best blend of light colors, equip each shop lite with one "warm white" fluorescent tube and one "cool white" tube.

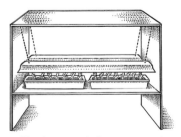

STEP TWO: This homemade frame—two side pieces and two shelves—is constructed from plywood or boards. When you first put seed-starting containers

on the bottom shelf, the light fixtures will need to hang two inches above the surface of the seed-starting mix. At this level, the heat from the fluorescent tubes will warm the mix just enough to encourage germination.

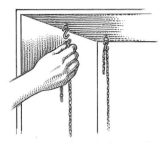

STEP THREE: Suspending the fixtures from chains hung from hooks screwed into the underside of the top shelf makes it easy to raise or lower the lights. Just unhook the chains and reattach higher or lower links.

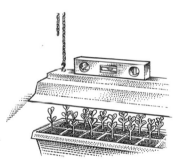

STEP FOUR: After germination, as your seedlings grow upward, raise the shop lites periodically to keep the fluorescent tubes a constant two inches above the seedlings' topmost leaves.

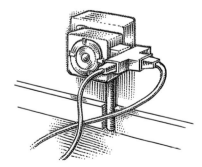

STEP FIVE: An electric light timer is a great convenience. Until germination occurs, the lights should stay on round the clock; but as soon as seedlings emerge, reduce the period of lighting to 16 hours a day.

PLASTIC CELL PACK

CLAY POT

PEAT POT

PLANT LABELS

PEAT CELL PACK

viola

CONTAINERS

BEFORE YOU CAN START seeds indoors, you need something to contain the seed-starting mix in which they will grow. Eventually, all gardeners develop their own preferences, as they identify the types of containers that work best with their personal style of growing and the kinds of plants they raise. The chart below spells out the advantages and disadvantages of each kind of container.

A key decision is whether to sow seeds in a "community" pot or in individual containers. With a community pot, you sow all the seeds from a packet into a single broad, shallow pan or tray, and later separate the seedlings that emerge and transplant them—prick them out—into individual containers.

Some gardeners prefer to sow right into the individual containers, dropping two seeds into each to ensure that at least one seedling emerges. If two seedlings appear in a single pot, one is snipped off at soil level. This method produces fewer seedlings per seed packet, but eliminates the time-consuming chore of pricking out.

Because seedlings are easy prey for bacteria and fungi, meticulous container hygiene is essential. Both plastic and terra-cotta containers must be cleaned thoroughly and disinfected before each use. Soaking them in a solution of nine parts water to one part chlorine bleach leaves containers pathogen free. You can do this in a large bucket, a garbage pail, or even the kitchen sink. Before immersing used containers, brush off any soil mix that still adheres to them. Then, after the containers are in the solution, scrub them with a bottle brush. Protect your hands from the bleach by wearing rubber gloves.

CONTAINER OPTIONS

TYPE OF CONTAINER	ADVANTAGES	DISADVANTAGES
PLASTIC POT	Inexpensive, durable, easy to clean; available in many sizes and shapes	Impermeable walls inhibit drainage, so prone to overwatering; not biodegradable
CLAY POT	Porous walls promote drainage, making clay less susceptible to overwatering than plastic; durable; available in many sizes and shapes	Expensive; easily broken; more difficult to clean than plastic; quick to dry out
PLASTIC CELL PACK	Inexpensive; easy-to-clean; models with four, six, eight, or more cells are available; ideal for large sowings of vegetables and flowers	Not durable—must usually be replaced after each use; not biodegradable; small size of individual cells makes them unsuitable for fast-growing, vigorous plants
PEAT PELLET	Naturally sterile, so doesn't need cleaning; because seedlings are transplanted pellet and all, transplanting shock is reduced, so ideal for plants with sensitive roots; biodegradable	Relatively expensive; must be replaced after each use; liable to get soggy and then dry out—careful watering a must; made from peat, a nonrenewable resource
PEAT POT	Naturally sterile, so doesn't need cleaning; because seedling is transplanted in pot, transplanting shock is minimal, so ideal for sensitive roots; biodegradable; easier to regulate watering than with pellet because change of pot color signals change in moisture	Relatively expensive; must be replaced after each use; liable to dry out unless individual pots are packed close together; made from peat, a nonrenewable resource

SEED-STARTING MIXES

HOWEVER GOOD garden soil may be, it is the wrong medium in which to start seeds indoors. The right mix, unlike soil, is sterile (pathogen free) and won't compact, remaining light and loose even after weeks in a container. In addition, the mix should absorb water easily but let excess moisture drain away quickly.

Many commercial mixes are excellent. Before buying any product, however, check the list of ingredients. Reject any mix that contains topsoil or compost: Both are likely to carry microorganisms, bacteria, and fungi that attack seeds and seedlings. If the mix includes peat, make sure it is sphagnum peat. This stable organic material efficiently absorbs and retains moisture and has a mildly antiseptic effect. Other kinds of peat are far less absorptive, and may supply only a fraction as much organic content.

So-called peat-lite mixtures—based on a combination of shredded sphagnum peat and horticultural vermiculite (expanded mica) or horticultural perlite (an expanded form of a volcanic rock) as well as a small dose of plant nutrients—are completely sterile. These provide an outstanding starting medium for most seeds.

HOMEMADE SEED-STARTING MIX It is easy to make a peat-lite mix. Begin by rubbing a bucketful of sphagnum peat through a coarse screen; a square of 1/4-inch wire mesh or "hardware cloth" stapled to a wooden frame works well as a sieve. Then mix one part sifted peat with one part vermiculite or one part perlite. Because this mix contains no plant nutrients, start fertilizing seedlings grown in it as soon as they have formed their true leaves (for fertilizer information, see Healthy Seedlings, page 32; for a definition of true leaves, see Seed Packet Translator, page 17).

JUST-IN-TIME SEED STARTING Good timing is critical for starting seeds indoors. Sow them too early, and the seedlings will end up pot-bound and stunted before they can be planted out. Sowing too late results in a delayed harvest, or maybe no harvest at all: Spring-blooming annuals that are sown too late won't mature enough to flower before summer heat cuts down the plants.

Careful scheduling also helps you make better use of precious indoor growing space—you can start English daisies early, for example, then move those seedlings out into the garden to create space under the lights for a flat of tomatoes. Photocopy the worksheet on the facing page, and write in the average date of the last spring frost in your area. Seed packets and our Plant Glossary (page 60) will tell you how many weeks before that date each type of seed should be sown.

FILLING A CELL PACK

SOWING IN A POT

DATE OF LAST FROST			
TYPE OF SEED (species, cultivar)	SOWING DATE (weeks before last frost)	PLANTING OUT DATE	NOTES
Brandywine Tomato	6-8 weeks	May 15th	Cover Seeds

YOU'VE ASSEMBLED all the ingredients and made all your preparations, and now the moment has finally come: It's time to open the packets and sow the seeds. This is one of the pleasantest rituals of a gardener's spring (and it's one worth repeating at intervals throughout the year). There's always the promise of something new, but the routine remains reassuringly the same. In fact, you'll apply the same basic treatment to all your indoor sowings, with only slight adjustments depending on the type of seed.

PREPARING CONTAINERS: Pour enough seed-starting mix to fill your containers into a pail or dishpan. Don't fill it right to the brim: Mixes can scatter if not confined. Add hot water, a cupful at a time, working it in with your fingers, until the mix is evenly moist but not wet; it should feel like a moistened and wrung-out sponge.

Cover the drainage holes in clay or plastic pots with a single thickness of newspaper so the mix won't leak out; peat pots and pellets and cell packs don't need this treatment. Fill pots, trays, or packs to the top of the lip with the moistened mix. Brush off any excess.

Using the bottom of an identical pot, gently tamp down the mix in the first container. Children's wooden blocks do the trick for trays. Don't pack the mix too tightly, because this can impede root growth—that's why Martha uses her fingertips to tamp down cell packs. The surface of the mix should be firm and level, and a half inch below the top of the container's lip.

DISTRIBUTING SEEDS: The technique differs, depending on whether seeds are to be sown in individual containers or in a community pot, but the goal remains the same: to distribute seeds evenly, leaving no area under the fluorescent lights unplanted and yet allowing each seedling space to develop. Crowded seedlings grow tall and weak, and are prone to damping off (for more on damping off see pages 16, 28, and 32).

Before You Sow

SEED PRETREATMENTS

SOME SEEDS NEED A PUSH TO GET THEM STARTED, BUT DO JUST FINE ONCE THEY GET GOING. TWO KINDS OF TREATMENT YOU CAN GIVE SUCH SEEDS BEFORE YOU SOW THEM—SCARIFICATION AND PRESOAKING—MAY INCREASE THE CHANCE THAT THEY WILL SPROUT AND ACCELERATE THEIR GERMINATION. PRETREATMENTS ARE RECOMMENDED, WHERE APPROPRIATE, IN THE PLANT GLOSSARY.

SCARIFICATION

Nature encases some seeds, such as those of nasturtiums, morning glories, and moonflowers, in a hard, impermeable coat. For these seeds to germinate, the coat must be punctured, allowing water and oxygen to reach the embryo inside. The natural process of decay might eventually accomplish the same result, but you can guarantee it by scarifying the seeds before sowing. The simplest, and safest, way to do this is to rub the seeds back and forth a couple of times across a sheet of medium-fine sandpaper (see photo, page 45). Remember: The goal is to nick the seed coat, not to remove it.

PRESOAKING

Some seeds, especially large ones or those with hard seed coats, are slow to absorb the moisture they need to germinate. Others contain natural chemicals that keep the seeds dormant until these substances dissolve and wash away. In either case, germination can be given a boost by soaking the seeds in warm water (not hot) overnight before planting them. After soaking, drain off the water, taking care not to lose the seeds. Sow them immediately. Small seeds may stick together when wet and therefore be hard to handle; mix them with a handful of clean, dry sand before sowing. Seeds that benefit from presoaking include parsley, carrots, corn, morning glories, New Zealand spinach, and sweet peas.

MOISTENING THE MIX

FILLING CELL PACKS

TAMPING DOWN THE MIX

DISTRIBUTING SEEDS

When sowing into individual containers, deposit two seeds on the surface of the mix at the center of each pot or cell. When sowing into a community pot, scatter seeds over the entire surface of the mix. The space you leave between seeds varies with their size. Sow small seeds (such as those of snapdragons and petunias) a quarter-inch apart, medium ones (tomatoes and marigolds) a half-inch apart, and large ones (black-eyed Susans and nasturtiums) one full inch apart—sometimes more, as in the case of beet seeds, which are actually balls of two to six individual seeds.

A good way to distribute seeds is to open the top flap or cut the top off the packet, turn it on its side, and gently tap the seeds out, one by one. You may prefer to pour large seeds into a saucer or the palm of one hand and drop them into place one by one with the fingers of the other. Combine fine, dustlike seeds with a handful of clean, fine sand and place in an empty salt shaker to sprinkle evenly over the mix (see Sprinkling Seeds, page 45). **COVERING SEEDS:** Seed packets and the Plant Glossary (page 60) indicate which seeds germinate best in darkness, as is the case with calendula and bachelor's button. To block the light, cover the seeds with an extra sifting of dry starting mix after you sow. Use dry mix for this step. When sowing seeds you know are prone to damping off, cover them with a layer of clean sand rather than starting mix. Martha covers all seeds with No. 2-grade coarse sand, unless they are varieties that require light to germinate or are very fine.

The rule of thumb is to cover seeds to a depth equal to three times their diameter. Don't worry about being exact; your seeds won't mind being buried a bit too shallow or too deep. If the seed packet and the Plant Glossary indicate that seeds need exposure to light to germinate, don't cover them. Press them lightly into the surface of the starting mix.

LABELING CONTAINERS: With an indelible marker, write the name of the seed and the date of sowing onto a plastic or wooden plant label; slide the tip of the label between the starting mix and the side of the container. Save the empty seed packets; the information they provide will be useful after your seedlings move out into the garden.

WATERING: A heavy spray of water that floods the surface of the starting mix will wash carefully distributed seeds into corners. Instead, water from the bottom by setting containers in an inch of water in a dishpan. Leave the containers in the water until moisture has crept up to darken the surface of the seed-starting mix. If you prefer to water from the top, merely moisten the surface of the mix with a plant mister (an old window-cleaner spray bottle works well, if thoroughly cleaned first).

COVERING CONTAINERS: To keep seeds and starting mix evenly moist during germination, cover containers with clear plastic before placing them under fluorescent lights. Many seed-starting kits include a rigid plastic cover. If your containers are not equipped with covers, just slip them inside a clear plastic bag. Don't seal the bag, because germinating seeds need fresh air. Check inside the bag periodically to make sure the mix is still moist, and water it as necessary. If mold starts to grow on the mix, remove the bag.

GERMINATION: Check your seed containers daily. As soon as the first green shoots appear, remove the plastic bags. Take care, however, to keep the seed-starting mix moist until germination is completed and the emergence of new seedlings slows markedly or stops altogether.

If, despite your best efforts, community pots become overcrowded, snip off any excess seedlings at soil level with a pair of embroidery scissors. Similarly, if

WATERING FROM BELOW

PLASTIC COVERS

REMOVING SEEDLINGS

PRICKING OUT

TRANSPLANTED SEEDLINGS

MISTING TRANSPLANTS

both of the seeds sown in a smaller pot have germinated, snip out the smaller, weaker seedling.

PRICKING OUT: As soon as the seedlings in community pots have produced true leaves (for a definition of true leaves, see Seed-Packet Translator, page 17), it is time to prick them out; that is, transfer them to individual pots or to cell packs.

Begin by filling the pots or cell packs with moist starting mix. Poke a sharp pencil into the center of each pot or cell and wiggle it to make a conical hole. Then, with the tip of a plant label, a skewer, or a table knife, lift a

clump of seedlings out of the community pot and set them down on a table. Use the pencil point to tease apart the roots, so that you can separate the seedlings.

Carefully grasp a seedling by one leaf (never seize it by the stem) and lower the roots into one of the conical holes. Use the tip of the pencil or label to gently push the surrounding starting mix in around the seedling's roots. When you have finished replacing each clump of seedlings, gently water the pots or cell packs of new transplants to further settle the starting mix and moisten the disturbed roots. Then go back for another seedling.

SNAPDRAGON

TOMATO

STRAWFLOWER

SWEET BASIL

MEALY SAGE

CHINA ASTER

EGGPLANT

PEPPER

CABBAGE

ZINNIA

HOW MANY IS ENOUGH?

A GARDENER'S NATURAL inclination is to sow all the seeds in a packet—but do you really want to contend with fifty tomato plants? The chart on this page is designed to help you plan more realistic sowings. It suggests quantities for ten of the most popular vegetables and cut flowers that are commonly started indoors.

With a bit of extrapolation, it is easy to fill in boxes for similar plants not listed here. This list gives the number of seedlings you will need, not the number of seeds you should sow. It is wise to start more seeds than the number of plants you'll ultimately require, since some seeds may not germinate.

EDIBLES	NUMBER OF SEEDLINGS FOR A HOUSEHOLD OF ONE OR TWO	NUMBER OF SEEDLINGS FOR A FAMILY OF FOUR
CABBAGE (*Brassica oleracea*)	8 of small-headed cultivars (a single variety or a mix) such as 'Earliana' or 'Salad Delight' for spring planting; start 12 Chinese cabbage seedlings—'Two Seasons' is a good variety— in late summer for fall stir-fries	20 standard-heading cabbages, in a mix of early-, mid- and late-season cultivars (varieties developed through cultivation) for spring planting; 20 Chinese cabbage seedlings for late-summer and fall planting
EGGPLANT (*Solanum melongena*)	3 of early-bearing cultivars such as 'Black Beauty' or 'Applegreen' in the North; a mix of early- and late-bearing cultivars such as 'Louisiana Long Green' in the South	6, in a mix of European-style cultivars such as 'Rosa Bianca' with Asian, long-fruited cultivars such as 'Rosita'; early or late bearing, depending on garden location
PEPPER (*Capsicum annuum*)	6 of bell peppers such as 'Chocolate'; 6 sweet roasting or frying peppers such as 'Cubanelle'; 6 hot peppers such as 'Jalapeño M' or 'Thai Dragon'	12 bell, 12 frying, 12 hot peppers
SWEET BASIL (*Ocimum basilicum*)	1, for culinary seasoning and salads; 6 of large-leaved cultivars such as 'Genovese,' to be used in pesto	1 to 2, for seasoning and salads; 12 large-leaved cultivars, for pesto
TOMATO (*Lycopersicon esculentum*)	2 cherry tomatoes; 6 indeterminate (see the Plant Glossary, page 108) beefsteak or standard slicing tomatoes (2 early-bearing, 2 midseason, 2 late-bearing cultivars); 6 determinate plum or paste tomatoes, for sauces and soups	2 cherry tomatoes; 9 indeterminate slicing tomatoes (3 early-bearing, 3 midseason, 3 late-bearing); 10 determinate plum tomatoes, for sauces, soups, and canning

FLOWERS	NUMBER OF SEEDLINGS FOR TWO BOUQUETS A WEEK	
CHINA ASTER (*Callistephus chinensis*)	24 in a mix of flower colors; at a 10-inch spacing, these will fill a 4-by-5-foot block	
MEALY SAGE (*Salvia farinacea*)	9 of violet-blue-flowered cultivar 'Victoria,' 9 of white-and-blue flowered 'Strata'	
SNAPDRAGON (*Antirrhinum majus*)	36 tall cultivars in a mix of colors; at an 8-inch spacing, these will fill a 3-by-3 foot space; in the South, replant in early fall for late-fall or early-winter flowers	
STRAWFLOWER (*Helichrysum bracteatum*)	20; at a 12-inch spacing, these will fill a 3-by-5-foot patch; dry and save cut stems for winter bouquets; combine with dried lavender spikes or branches of rosemary for fragrant winter bouquets	
ZINNIA (*Zinnia elegans*)	48; at a 12-inch spacing, these will fill a 3-by-9-foot plot; heirloom, open-pollinated 'Pulcino' and 'Pumila' offer long, sturdy stems and mixed flower colors; ideal for cutting; 'Envy' has striking chartreuse flowers	

HEALTHY SEEDLINGS

LIGHTING: Give seedlings sixteen hours of light daily; frequently raise fluorescent fixtures so that the tubes remain two inches above the topmost leaves. Martha periodically rotates trays and cell packs to make sure that seedlings near the outer edges of the containers don't stretch to reach the light.

VENTILATION: Set a small electric fan near pots or trays of seedlings to keep the air gently circulating. Adequate ventilation encourages sturdy seedling growth, and protects the tender plants against damping off and other diseases (see Seed-Packet Translator, Damping Off, page 16).

WATERING: Water only when the seed-starting mix dries. To check the moisture level, touch the surface of the mix with a fingertip or heft the container— dry containers are lighter than moist ones. Water the mix with a gentle spray from a watering can with a water breaker or "rose" screwed onto the spout.

FERTILIZATION: Seedlings grown in homemade peat-lite mixes need to be fertilized as soon as the true leaves appear. Apply water-soluble fertilizer with a balanced nutrient formula (such as 20-20-20, standard code for 20 percent nitrogen, 20 percent phosphorus, and 20 percent potash) or fish emulsion; use either at half the rate recommended by the manufacturer. Fertilize weekly thereafter. Commercial seed-starting mixes contain fertilizer; weekly feedings aren't needed until a month after pricking out.

HARDENING OFF

AFTER BEING RAISED in a carefully controlled indoor environment, your tender seedlings will collapse if they are suddenly exposed to the garden's more strenuous conditions. Prepare the seedlings for this transition with the gradual process of acclimatization known as hardening off.

Begin two weeks before you plan to plant out seedlings in the garden, on a day when the temperature rises above fifty degrees. Set the containers of seedlings outdoors for just an hour or two, in a spot sheltered from the wind and where the sunlight is filtered by overhead branches. Over succeeding days, increase the time that the seedlings remain outdoors by an hour or so every day. If they are sun-loving plants, you should gradually expose them to more intense light, too, by moving them out from under the canopy of branches.

Leave the seedlings indoors on chilly days (when the temperature in the garden stays below fifty degrees), and resume hardening off when the weather warms. By the second week's end, the seedlings should be staying outdoors all day and all night, and will be ready for their ultimate move to the garden.

SEED STORAGE

YOU BOUGHT THE BEST SEED from a reliable supplier, yet if you stored it improperly after you took it home, you may end up with a disappointing sowing. Leave newly purchased seeds out in the potting shed for several weeks, and their vitality will decline markedly; stashing them in a kitchen drawer is not much better.

Proper seed storage begins with an air-tight, resealable container. One-quart canning jars with screw-on lids are ideal, and an empty peanut butter jar is a close runner-up. To reduce the humidity inside the jar, cover the bottom with a half-inch layer of dry silica gel—this is the material inside the desiccant packs shipped with electronic equipment such as computers and cameras. Actually, you can re-use the desiccant packs from your last purchase if you first dry them out by placing them in a 200° oven for eight hours. Or buy the gel from a craft-supply store.

Afterward, put the seed packets into the jar (Martha likes to label jars by plant category, such as perennials or vegetables, and group packets accordingly). Screw on the lid to create a tight seal. Then place the jar in the refrigerator. Stored this way, seeds will be as good at planting time as they were when they left the nursery. And those half-empty packets, left over after you've filled every inch of the garden? Repack them, put them back in the refrigerator, and they will keep until fall planting time.

STARTING SEEDS
IN THE GARDEN

PART 2

Long before

there were fluorescent lights or even windowsills in heated rooms, there were gardens, and the vegetables, herbs, and flowers in those ancestral plots were all "direct sown." That is, the seeds were planted directly into the ground, usually in the same spot where the resulting plants were intended to grow. This worked for our forebears centuries ago, and it works just as well today—because direct sowing is not only the simplest way to start seeds, for many plants it is by far the best

way. Poppies, peas, beans, and nasturtiums are only a few of the plants whose roots are easily damaged during transplanting, and which usually grow better if direct sown. In addition, there is a host of other plants whose seeds may be started equally well indoors or out. If you have no reason for getting a head start on the season, you will find it less work to sow these "either-or" seeds right into the garden soil and skip the tasks of pricking out, hardening off, and transplanting.

BETTING ON DIRECT SOWING

It's true, direct sowing is a bit of a gamble. In an outdoor setting, the seeds and seedlings are far more vulnerable to hungry birds and insects, or to an unseasonable cold snap. But by taking a few simple precautions, you can minimize the risks (see Troubleshooting, page 52). A few disappointments are inevitable, but when you win, the payoff can be impressive. Because most of us have far more space for planting out-of-doors than in, direct sowing allows us to plant in far greater numbers, ensuring bigger harvests of flowers, vegetables, and fruits. With more room to cultivate, we can also experiment with a greater variety of plants, trying out unknowns and novelties that, perhaps, we could not afford to sow in our limited indoor growing area.

DESIGNING AS YOU SOW

Direct sowing does involve some techniques different from those used for indoor seed starting. For example, indoor seedlings are planted in an arrangement designed primarily to make maximum use of the available growing space. When direct sowing, on the other hand, you must keep in mind the spacing the mature plant will require, and try to visualize what

sort of arrangement will be attractive then. After all, though you will probably thin your direct-sown plantings, you won't transplant them, and so there will be plants only where you have put seeds.

A couple of generations ago, when the fashion for massed bedding displays demanded huge numbers of precisely spaced plants, gardeners also made outdoor sowings in a special nursery bed. They'd raise seedlings there and later transplant them to where they were wanted in the garden. However, because this method combines all the work of indoor seed-starting with all the hazards of direct sowing, it is rarely used today.

SCHEDULING SOWINGS

Timing can be somewhat more complex when you direct sow. Besides scheduling around the average dates of the local last and first frosts, the gardener who direct sows has to consult the weather as well. If, for instance, spring is slow to arrive, and the weather stays frosty after it would normally have begun to warm, you should delay sowing—even if the calendar shows the correct number of weeks left before the last frost. Likewise, a rainy spell may leave the soil too soggy to be dug, forcing you to wait for the damp ground to drain.

RESPECTING REGIONAL DIFFERENCES

The decision whether to a sow a particular flower or vegetable indoors or out depends partly on that plant's needs—an annual flower native to the tropics, for example, may need a longer growing season than your climate provides, and so require that you start it early, indoors. But the choice of sowing style, also depends on where you garden. In the North, with its short summers, tomatoes must be sown indoors if they are to mature and bear fruit before summer's end. In the Deep South, however, where the growing season is long, tomatoes may be direct sown, though most gardeners also start some seedlings indoors to guarantee an earlier harvest.

In the North, it's general practice to start the seeds of cool-weather-loving annual flowers, such as snapdragons and calendulas, indoors in late winter. This ensures that the plants, which collapse in summer heat, will have time to mature and blossom during the brief Northern spring. Southern gardeners commonly sow these same plants into the garden in midfall, because their region's cool (but not frigid) weather in fall, winter, and spring provides plenty of time for cool-loving annuals to mature.

The chart on pages 40–41 gives a list of flowers and vegetables that are usually direct sown, either because the seedlings resent transplanting or because the plants grow so quickly that an indoor head start is unnecessary. Recommendations on what and what not to direct sow are also included in the Plant Glossary (page 60). However, you should make a point of consulting with experienced gardeners in your neighborhood, or with an agent at the local Cooperative Extension office. Climate can change significantly in a half-hour's drive, so that what works for gardeners in the next county, even if it lies within the same USDA plant-hardiness zone (see the zone map on page 47), may not work for you. The best gardening advice is always local.

Timing

SIGNALS FOR WHEN TO DIRECT SOW

AS SOON AS THE SOIL CAN BE WORKED: This phrase is commonly used to describe an early spring sowing. In very early spring, your garden soil may still be frozen and therefore impossible to dig or cultivate (to "work"). Right after it has thawed, however, the soil is likely to be so wet that any digging or cultivation will compact it into muck. But once the soil has thawed and dried—if you squeeze a ball of it in your hand, it should crumble when you poke it with a fingertip—then it is ready to be worked, and ready for early sowings.

AS SOON AS THE SOIL HAS WARMED: Some seeds won't germinate unless the soil is warm; if planted into cold soils, they are likely to rot. Squash seeds, for example, need a soil temperature of approximately 65°, and their seed packets routinely advise delaying sowing "until the soil has warmed." Other seeds that require warm soils include castor beans, sweet corn, cucumbers, and melons. A temperature of 60-65° is adequate for all of these. An inexpensive soil thermometer, sold by garden centers and greenhouse-supply companies, is the best tool for measuring soil temperature. For the most accurate reading, test in the morning when the soil is coolest, and push the thermometer probe two inches below the surface.

WHEN ALL DANGER OF FROST IS PAST: Because the last frost date (see Seed-Packet Translator, page 17) is an average date, there is always some danger of frost in the days immediately following it. For this reason, the instructions on seed packets and in this book's Plant Glossary often recommend waiting to plant out particularly cold-sensitive varieties until "all danger of frost is past." To ascertain that date, consult your Cooperative Extension office, local nurseries, or experienced gardeners in your area.

STARTING SEEDS IN THE GARDEN

PLANT	DIRECT SOWING DATE	NOTES
ALYSSUM (*Lobularia maritima*)	After danger of frost is past	Can also be sown indoors 5 weeks before transplanting outdoors
ARUGULA (*Eruca vesicaria* var. *sativa*)	As soon as soil can be worked	Make small sowings every second week through midspring for a prolonged harvest; sow again in fall
BABY BLUE-EYES (*Nemophila menziesii*)	As soon as soil can be worked	In mild climates, sow in fall for winter and spring bloom
BACHELOR'S BUTTON (*Centaurea cyanus*)	After danger of frost is past	Where winters are mild, sow again in fall
BEET (*Beta vulgaris*)	2–3 weeks before last frost date	
CALENDULA (*Calendula officinalis*)	After danger of frost is past	Seed can also be started indoors, 3–4 weeks before last frost; in frost-free areas, sow again in fall
CALIFORNIA POPPY (*Eschscholzia californica*)	After danger of frost is past	Where winters are mild, it will self-sow
CARROT (*Daucus carota*)	1–2 weeks before last spring frost	
CILANTRO (*Coriandrum sativum*)	As soon as soil can be worked	Where winters are mild, sow again in fall
CLARKIA (*Clarkia* spp.)	As soon as soil can be worked	Where winters are mild, sow again in late summer through fall
CLEOME (*Cleome hassleriana*)	As soon as soil can be worked	Plants are annuals but self-sow, producing new crops of seedlings every spring
COREOPSIS (*Coreopsis tinctoria*)	As soon as soil can be worked	
CORN (*Zea mays*)	When danger of frost has past and soil has warmed	Make small plantings at 10–14 day intervals to prolong harvest and keep pickings manageable
COSMOS (*Cosmos* spp.)	When all danger of frost is past	For earlier flowering, start seeds indoors 4–6 weeks before last frost
CUCUMBER (*Cucumis sativus*)	7–10 days after last frost	
DILL (*Anethum graveolens*)	As soon as soil can be worked	Sow again in late summer for a fall crop
FENNEL (*Foeniculum vulgare*)	When danger of frost is past	
FORGET-ME-NOT (*Myosotis sylvatica*)	As soon as soil can be worked	Where winters are mild, sow again in fall for spring color

PLANT	DIRECT SOWING DATE	NOTES
LARKSPUR (*Consolida ambigua*)	As soon as soil can be worked	Where winters are mild, sow from fall to early spring
LETTUCE (*Lactuca sativa*)	As soon as soil can be worked	To prolong the harvest, make small sowings every 10 days throughout spring
LOVE-IN-A-MIST (*Nigella damascena*)	After danger of frost is past	Where winters are mild, sow again in fall
MARIGOLD (*Tagetes* spp.)	When all danger of frost is past	Triploid hybrids of African marigold (*T. erecta*) and French marigold (*T. patula*) have low rate of germination and should be sown indoors 4–6 weeks before last frost
MORNING GLORY (*Ipomoea nil*)	After last frost, as soon as soil warms	May also be started indoors 2–3 weeks before last frost
NASTURTIUM (*Tropaeolum majus*)	When danger of frost is past	May also be started indoors 4 weeks before last frost
OKRA (*Abelmoschus esculentus*)	When soil has warmed	In North, may be started indoors about the time of last frost; plant out when soil has warmed
PEA (*Pisum sativum*)	As soon as soil can be worked	In the South and West where winters are mild, sow again in fall or early winter
POPPY (*Papaver commutatum*)	As soon as soil can be worked in spring, or fall	Where winters are severe, start indoors in midwinter and plant out when danger of frost is past
PUMPKIN (*Cucurbita pepo*)	After last spring frost	
RADISH (*Raphanus sativus*)	Make small sowings of spring radishes at 2-week intervals, beginning as soon as soil can be worked; continue until midspring	Sow winter radishes (also known as daikon) in late summer (in the South, in early fall) for a fall or winter harvest
SNAP BEAN (*Phaseolus vulgaris*)	As soon as soil warms to 60 degrees	Sow again in mid to late summer for a fall crop
SPINACH (*Spinacia oleracea*)	As soon as soil can be worked	Where summers are cool, make a second sowing 2 weeks after the first; where winters are mild, sow again in late summer or early fall
SUMMER SQUASH (*Cucurbita pepo*)	Midspring, around last frost date	
SUNFLOWER (*Helianthus annuus*)	When danger of frost is past	
SWEET PEA (*Lathyrus odoratus*)	As soon as soil can be worked	Where winters are mild, sow again in late fall for early spring bloom
SWISS CHARD (*Beta vulgaris* var. *flavescens*)	When danger of frost is past	

STARTING SEEDS OUTDOORS is a simple process, but every step matters: The gardener provides the seeds' only defense against nature's uncertainties. You can't stop a week of rainy weather, for example, but if you prepared the soil carefully, so that it drains well, your seeds won't drown.

The planting style you choose is important, too. Traditionally, direct-sown vegetables and flowers have been planted in evenly spaced rows. This ensures that each plant has ample room to spread its roots as it grows. It also makes it easy to keep the garden weed free by hoeing the surface of the soil between rows. Today, however, many gardeners prefer to sow in blocks: They "broadcast" the seed, sprinkling it evenly over the surface of a bed, in blocks up to three feet wide, and then work it into the soil with a hand cultivator (this works especially well with shallowly sown vegetable seeds such as lettuce or arugula). Because it leaves no soil unplanted, broadcasting makes more efficient use of precious garden space. In the flower garden, this technique lends itself to the creation of large flowing "drifts" of color. Weeds must be pulled by hand, although with less vacant space for them to invade, there are fewer of them. And the uninterrupted canopy of foliage shades the soil, serving as a living mulch in summertime to keep the soil cooler.

Bring a sample of your soil to the local Cooperative Extension office and have a complete soil test carried out by its laboratory technicians. Though such a test costs only a few dollars, its results furnish an exact prescription for the fertilizer, lime, organic matter, or other amendments your garden beds need to nurture healthy seed and plant growth.

PREPARING THE SOIL: With a spading fork, dig the soil in your bed to a depth of at least eight inches (a depth of twelve inches is better). Break up the soil clods, and remove stones and weed roots. Then broadcast over the soil's surface the amendments called for by the results of the soil test. Even if you have not tested the soil, at least enrich it with compost, which benefits any garden soil. Spread the compost over the beds in a layer two inches thick.

After spreading the compost and other soil amendments (if any), dig them in by turning the soil again with a spading fork. Then smooth the soil with a rake (opposite, top). Use the rake to remove any pebbles or twigs and break up remaining clods.

SOWING IN ROWS: With stakes and strings, mark planting rows on the bed, spacing them at the intervals noted on the seed packets or in the Plant Glossary. Draw one corner of a hoe blade along the ground under each string, opening a furrow of the depth recommended for that particular kind of seed on the packet or in this book's Plant Glossary. For tiny seeds, such as lettuce, Martha simply lays the handle of a hoe or rake on the soil and presses down to make a shallow furrow (opposite, center).

Next, drop the seeds along the bottom of the furrow, again observing the recommended spacing. Always sow the seeds more closely than you want the mature plants to stand. The germination rate of direct-sown seeds is relatively low, so you'll need the extra seedlings to avoid gaps in the row when the seedlings emerge. Where seedlings are crowded, you can thin.

With a sifting of soil or clean sand, cover seeds to the depth specified by seed packets and the Plant Glossary. Sand has the advantage that it doesn't crust over, so seedlings meet less resistance as they emerge. Or use an old rule-of-thumb: Cover a seed to a depth equal to three times its diameter.

After sowing each packet of seed, write the plant name and sowing date with an indelible marker on two plastic, wooden, or metal labels, and place one at each end of the row before moving on to your next sowing.

SMOOTHING THE SOIL WITH A RAKE

MAKING FURROWS WITH A RAKE HANDLE

SOWING IN A FURROW

SOWING IN BLOCKS: Mark the borders of planting blocks on the surface of the raked beds with a line of garden lime dribbled between your fingers. Blocks should be no more than four feet wide, enabling you to reach into the center without stepping on the planted area. If the soil surface has crusted, loosen it with a hand cultivator. Then sprinkle seeds evenly over the soil surface. Space them so that the interval between seeds is equal to the distance the seed packet recommends for spacing seeds within a row; ignore the interval recommended for separating rows.

After distributing the seeds evenly across the bed, cover them with a thin layer of sifted compost, or work them in by scratching the soil back and forth lightly with the hand cultivator. Then label the block, again recording the type of seed and the sowing date.

SOWING IN HILLS: A few vining fruit and vegetable crops, such as melons and squashes, are usually planted in circles of seeds, called hills (photo below right). Four or five seeds are planted in a ring twelve inches across; you'll find the proper spacing between hills on the seed packet or in the Plant Glossary. After germination, remove all but the two sturdiest seedlings from each hill.

PROTECTING SOWN SEEDS: Water the bed with a fine spray of water from a hose or watering can, enough to thoroughly moisten the top couple of inches of soil. Then cover the row or block with a "floating row cover." Made from light, porous translucent-plastic fabric, a row cover filters the sun and blocks the wind, keeping the soil underneath moister and slightly warmer than uncovered beds, and thus aiding germination. Row covers also keep birds and flying insects from feeding on seeds and seedlings.

Drape the row-cover material loosely over the planted area, leaving plenty of slack so that the emerging seedlings can push the fabric upward (that's how the row cover "floats"). Then dig a trench a few inches deep around the perimeter of the planted area, tuck the edges of the row cover into the trench, and bury them with the loosened soil to anchor it. In the flower garden, a row cover should be taken off as soon as the seedlings have produced a couple of true leaves. In the vegetable garden, a cover may stay in place until the onset of hot weather, or until fruiting plants such as squashes start to flower, at which time the cover must be removed to let pollinators reach the blossoms.

THINNING SEEDLINGS: If all goes well, most of the seeds you have sown will germinate. The result will be a row or block that is overcrowded. Thin by pulling out excess seedlings, so that the remainder stand at the intervals recommended on the seed packet or in the Plant Glossary. It is important to thin while the seedlings are still small, before they develop extensive root systems; that way, in pulling one you won't disrupt its neighbors. Martha uses thinnings from beets to flavor stocks and soups, and to add a delicate crunch to salads. She puts other pulled seedlings on the compost heap or feeds them to her chickens.

SOWING IN A HILL

SCARIFYING A SEED   ADDING SEEDS TO SAND   SPRINKLING SEEDS

Helping Seeds to Succeed

SIGNALS FOR WHEN TO DIRECT SOW

SCARIFICATION

To encourage the germination of seeds with hard waterproof coats, such as those of morning glories and nasturtiums, you should puncture their coats. Rub the seed across medium-fine sand paper to nick the coat (photo above left; see page 26 for more on scarification).

SPRINKLING SEEDS

Extremely fine seeds, such as those of poppies and cleome, are difficult to distribute evenly when grasped between your fingers or tapped out of an open packet. To sow these seeds more effeciently, make a seed shaker from a jelly jar (photos above center and right). Using a sharp-pointed nail, punch small holes in the metal lid. Place a few tablespoonfuls of coarse washed sand in the jar, add the contents of a seed packet, and swirl the jar or stir to mix sand and seed. Screw on the lid and shake the mix over prepared soil. Gently tap the mix into the soil with your hand or an inverted cultivator.

KEEPING SEEDS WARM

To warm the soil for heat-loving vegetable or fruit crops, cover the planting area with black plastic mulch just before planting time (water the planting area well before covering). Then stretch the plastic film taut, and anchor it by burying the edges under soil. At planting time, sow the seeds through crisscrosses of four-inch-long slits cut into the plastic with a sharp knife.

TEMPERING SUN

When sowing outdoors during summer or other periods of hot, sunny weather, how do you keep the seeds from cooking? After planting, water and then cover each row with lengths of 2"x6" scrap lumber. Shelter block sowings with sheets of plywood set off the ground atop bricks. Check underneath the boards or plywood every morning and remove them at the first signs of germination.

BREAKING HARD SOIL

Because the soil may crust over slow-to-germinate seeds such as carrots, the seedlings may have trouble breaking through into sunlight and air. Guard against this by planting radish seeds into the row of carrots at six-inch intervals. The radish seeds germinate in days, marking the row where the other crop is planted and breaking the soil crust in the process. Later, when you harvest the mature radishes, you will get a head start on thinning their slower rowmates.

GOOD GARDENERS KNOW that spring planting is just the beginning: Summer and fall—and, in the subtropical south, winter—are planting seasons, too. If you don't take advantage of these multiseasonal opportunities for direct sowing, you are missing half, or more, of the rewards your garden has to offer.

SUMMER PLANTINGS: Throughout most of the Northeast and the upper Midwest, the second planting season begins with the onset of summer. Hot weather soon puts an end to the cool-weather-loving annuals planted in early spring. Pea vines wither, pansies peter out, and lettuce bolts (produces flowers instead of leafy heads). Fill the spots those plants vacate with late direct sowings of heat-loving annual flowers such as marigolds, zinnias, and cockscomb (*Celosia cristata*), or with transplants of the tropical annuals coleus, impatiens, and begonia.

The heat-loving vegetable seedlings you started indoors—peppers, tomatoes, and eggplants, for example—should then move out into the garden, to be tucked in with direct sowings of other heat-loving or heat-tolerant vegetables such as bush beans, the faster-maturing kinds of summer squashes, New Zealand spinach, and a last sowing of spring crops such as Swiss chard, beets, carrots, or corn.

Early summer is also the planting season for heat-loving vegetables in the coastal regions of southern California, where summers are sunny but not torrid. Gardeners in the cloudy, cool Pacific Northwest can sow summer vegetables and annual flowers then, or start a second generation of the cool-season crops, such as lettuces and snapdragons, that are traditional spring crops elsewhere.

The garden lies dormant throughout the summer in much of the Southeast and the desert Southwest, so autumn is the second planting season there. When the mercury starts to descend in September is the best time to sow cool-weather vegetable crops such as lettuce, spinach, cabbage, mustard greens, broccoli, or turnips and some cool-weather annuals such as calendula (pot marigold). Those plants will all flourish during the long interval before the southern winter arrives.

Gardeners in the milder regions of the northern states, the mid-Atlantic region, and the mountain South—upland North Carolina, Tennessee, Kentucky, and West Virginia—can carry out a similar second direct sowing, although they must pay closer attention to their scheduling. It's essential to check that enough days remain before the first autumn frost for newly planted seeds to mature and produce a crop.

COUNTING DAYS FOR A FALL CROP: This is easy to do. First check the "days to harvest" listed on the seed packet or in the Plant Glossary (see page 60). This figure reflects the number of days, on average, that the plant requires to develop from a newly sown seed to a harvestable size. Be sure to allow for extra time—because the days are growing shorter in the autumn, a late planting may exceed the listed number of days to maturity by as much as half.

Then consult a calendar. Count the days that would elapse between your desired sowing date (which should come after summer's heat has begun to cool) and the average date of the first fall frost in your part of the country (see Last Frost Date in the Seed-Packet Translator, page 17). If the number of available days exceeds the adjusted number of days to harvest, your climate can accommodate a late planting of that crop.

THE THIRD GROWING SEASON: In much of the Deep South and in the milder regions of the Southwest, there is yet a third planting season, in some respects the best of all. This is mid to late fall, and it is the ideal time for planting frost-tolerant annual vegetables and flowers such as winter lettuces, radicchio, peas, and cabbage; pansies, calendula, and sweet peas (*Lathyrus odoratus*). In a mild year, the fall-sown vegetables will begin to provide cuttings and pickings, and the flowers bloom, by midwinter. If the winter weather is relatively severe, the maturity of these plants may be delayed, but they will still supply the very earliest of early spring harvests and a welcome splash of color.

CHECKING THE ZONE MAP: As a guide to which plants can be grown successfully in a particular region, and when to direct sow their seeds, gardeners often refer to the United States Department of Agriculture Plant Hardiness Zone Map, below.

USDA PLANT HARDINESS ZONE MAP

THIS MAP DIVIDES THE COUNTRY INTO ELEVEN ZONES—1 BEING THE COLDEST AND 11 THE WARMEST—ACCORDING TO THE AVERAGE LOWEST ANNUAL TEMPERATURE IN EACH REGION (THOSE MINIMUM TEMPERATURES APPEAR BESIDE THE COLOR-CODED ZONE KEY AT LOWER RIGHT). THESE ZONES PROVIDE ONLY GENERAL GUIDELINES. WIND, HUMIDITY, SUMMER SUNSHINE, SOIL TYPE, AND OTHER FACTORS MAY ALSO AFFECT PLANT HARDINESS.

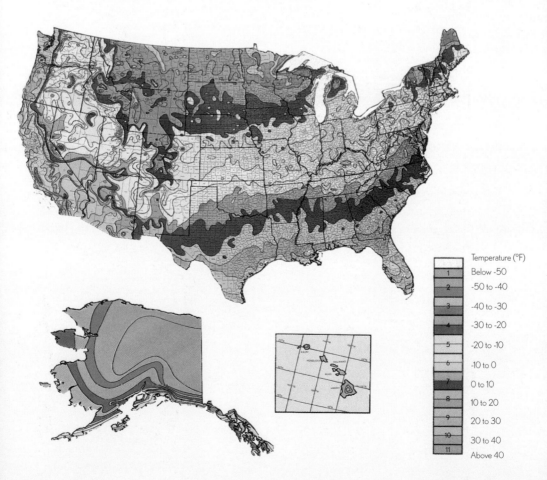

Zone	Temperature (°F)
1	Below -50
2	-50 to -40
3	-40 to -30
4	-30 to -20
5	-20 to -10
6	-10 to 0
7	0 to 10
8	10 to 20
9	20 to 30
10	30 to 40
11	Above 40

ONION

TOMATO

POPPY

PANSY

LETTUCE

LARKSPUR

CARROT

GLOBE AMARANTH

MARIGOLD

PEA

SECOND SOWINGS

The chart below and on pages 50-51 has been divided by season: summer, fall, and winter. Within each season, you'll find recommendations for vegetables and flowers that may be planted then. Because schedules vary with climate, we include information for five regions: Region A: Northeast and mid-Atlantic, upper Midwest, and Rocky Mountain West (USDA zones 3-7); Region B: Pacific Northwest (zones 6-9); Region C: Southern California, Southwest (zones 8 -10); Region D: Mountain South (North Carolina, Tennessee, Virginia, West Virginia, Kentucky–zones 6-7); Region E: Deep South and Hawaii (zones 7 to 10).

EARLY-MIDSUMMER SOWINGS		
PLANT	SOWING TIME	NOTES
BUSH BEAN	A: June–July; B: June–July; C: July–August; D: July	Black-eyed peas and crowder peas are good summer beans for the Southeast
CARROT	A: June–July; B: June–August; C: June–August; D: June–August	Short-rooted cultivars such as 'Thumbelina' are faster maturing and better in the North
COCKSCOMB	A: June; B: June; C: May–July; D: June; E: May–July	In hot summer areas, start later sowings indoors in peat pots and transplant out as weather cools
CORN	A: May–June; C: April–July; D: June–July; E: May–June	Early summer sowings of sweet corn are not advised north of zone 5
CUCUMBER	A: June; B: June–July; D: June	Cucumbers need warm weather to germinate, but do not flourish when summer temperatures rise into the 90s
GLOBE AMARANTH	A: June; B: May–June; C: April–July; D: June; E: May–July	In hot summer areas, start later sowings indoors in peat pots and transplant out as weather cools
LOVE-LIES-BLEEDING	A: June; B: June; C: May–July; D: June; E: May–June	In hot summer areas, start later sowings indoors in peat pots and transplant out as weather cools
MARIGOLD	A: June; B: June; C: May–July; D: June; E: May–July	In hot summer areas, start later sowings indoors in peat pots and transplant out as weather cools
ONION	B: June–August	Plant "long day" cultivars, which don't start making bulbs until each day's hours of light reach 14 to 16. "Short day" cultivars will turn to bulb production while plants are still too small
SWISS CHARD AND BEET	B: June–August	Late sowings escape spinach-leaf-miners, which commonly attack spring sowings
TOMATO	C: June; E: June–July	Start seeds indoors and use seedlings to replace heat-killed plants after midsummer; cold-tolerant cultivars such as 'Stupice' are best in the Southeast
ZINNIA	A: June; B: June; C: May–July D: June; E: May–July	In hot summer areas, start later sowings indoors in peat pots and transplant out as weather cools

PLANT	SOWING TIME	NOTES
BUSH BEAN	C: August-September; E: August-September	Snap beans are more tender and less stringy if grown as fall crop in the South
CABBAGE *(and other brassicas such as collards, kale, and turnip)*	A: July-August; B: August; C: August-October; D: July-August; E: September-October	In regions A, B, and D, check days to maturity on seed packets and schedule sowings so that the harvest comes around or before the first fall frost
CALENDULA	A: August; B: July-August; C: July; D: August; E: August-October	Direct sow into the garden for fall color
CARROT	B: August; C: August-October; D: August; E: September-October	Check days to maturity on seed packets and schedule sowings so that the harvest comes around or before the first fall frost
CUCUMBER	C: August-September; E: August-September	Soak seeds overnight before planting and cover sowings with scrap lumber until germination begins (see Tempering Sun, page 45)
LETTUCE AND SPINACH	A: August; B: August-September; C: August-October; D: August-September; E: September-October	In the North sow cold-hardy lettuce cultivars such as 'Arctic King,' 'Winter Marvel,' and 'Rouge d'Hiver'
ONION	A: August; C: September; D: August-September; E: August-October	Sow short-day cultivars such as 'Texas Early Grano 502' in the South; hardy bunching onions where winters are severe
PANSY *(and other hardy biennials such as hollyhock, sweet William, and Canterbury bells)*	A: July–mid-August; B: July–mid-August; C: July – mid-August; D: July–mid-August; E: August-September	Direct sow into a nursery bed and blanket with evergreen boughs over the winter; transplant to the garden in early spring
PEA	A: July; B: July; C: August-September; D: July	Bush peas are the easiest to cover, for protection from early frost
RADICCHIO	A: July-August; B: June-July; C: August-October; D: July-September; E: October	'Augusto,' 'Giulio,' and 'Early Treviso' are easy-to-grow cultivars
RADISH *(spring and winter types)*	A: August-October; B: August-October; C: September-October; D: September-October; E: October	In the North, mulch winter radishes with straw after the first frost; roots will sweeten and continue to gain bulk into winter
SNAPDRAGON	A: July; B: July-August; D: August-September; E: August-October	Start summer sowings indoors or in a shaded nursery bed, and transplant seedlings to garden

PLANT	SOWING TIME	NOTES
ALYSSUM	C: October-November; E: October	One of many cool season annual flowers that may be sown now
ANNUAL PHLOX	C: October-November; E: October	Planted now, this annual provides earliest spring bloom
BACHELOR'S BUTTON	C: October-November; E: October	In mildest climates, provides winter color; elsewhere in South, blooms in early spring
CARROT	C: October-December; E: October-December	Cover with straw mulch if frost threatens
COLLARDS, KALE, TURNIP	C: October-November; E: October-November	Winter harvests have the sweetest flavor
LARKSPUR (annual)	C: October-November; E: October-December	Make sowings into early December in the Southeast
LETTUCE AND SPINACH	C: October-December; E: October-December	In zone 7, grow in a cold frame
PEA	E: November-December	The latest plantings may be made in Florida
POPPY	C: October-November; E: October-December	Direct sow; poppies do not tolerate transplanting
RADICCHIO	C: October-December; E: October-December	In southern climates, radicchio grows best in the long, cool season of late fall and winter
RADISH	C: October-December; D: October; E: October-December	Sow winter radishes such as 'Black Spanish' or 'Chinese Rose' 90 days before fall frost; sow spring radishes ('Cherry Belle,' 'Easter Egg') until 30 days before frost
STOCK	C: October-November; E: October	Not winter-hardy in the coolest zones

TROUBLESHOOTING

YOUR SEEDS AREN'T GERMINATING, despite all the care you have given them. Seedlings are turning strange colors, looking half-eaten, or mysteriously disappearing. Or maybe they are just failing to thrive. Whatever it is, you've got problems.

Fortunately, because seeds' and seedlings' needs are few, the sources of trouble are also relatively few and generally easy to cure. If you got the basics right—prepared the soil well, chose types of seeds suited to the site, and sowed at an appropriate season—chances are you will find all you need to diagnose and treat your seed or seedling problem in this chart.

OUTDOOR PESTS AND DISEASES

PROBLEM	SYMPTOMS	CAUSE	TREATMENT
	Seedlings fail to emerge; soil surface feels hard	Soil surface has crusted over, suppressing seedling growth	Refrain from planting when soil is wet; cover sowings with No.2-grade coarse sand to help deter crusting
	Seedlings or transplants severed at base	Cutworms	Drench soil with beneficial nematode *Neoplectana carpocapsae* (ask your local Cooperative Extension for sources); surround the bases of seedling stems with collars of cardboard or aluminum foil, pushing base of collar down into soil
	Seedlings weak; leaves and buds stunted, distorted	Aphids	Spray seedlings with insecticidal soap or horticultural oil
	Leaves yellowing, dropping off; clouds of small white insects fly up when you brush seedling with hand or transplant it	Whitefly	Usually brought into garden on infested transplants; check carefully under leaves of seedlings at the nursery before purchasing. Trap flies on yellow cards coated with petroleum jelly or spray with insecticidal soap

PROBLEM	SYMPTOMS	CAUSE	TREATMENT
	Seeds dug up; newly sprouted seedlings uprooted or eaten	Birds; crows and blackbirds are especially fond of corn seed and seedlings	Foil birds with row covers (see page 44) or drape beds with fine plastic bird netting while seeds and seedlings are young and attractive
	Seedlings' leaves chewed; silvery trails on leaves and surrounding soil	Slugs or snails	Encircle planted area with broad bands of wood ash or lime; renew after rain. Leave scraps of lumber on surrounding soil; scrape hiding slugs off underside of lumber every morning
	Veins are green; leaves yellowing between	Possibly a result of sowing in mineral-deficient soil or of overwatering	Have soil tested; reduce frequency of watering, allowing soil to dry between irrigations
	Leaf margins and tips are dying	Leaf burn, often caused by salt in irrigation water or, in seaside gardens, by wind-driven salt spray	Call water utility and inquire about salt content of water; irrigate with rain water or use drip irrigation to reduce amount of water applied. Protect seaside gardens with windbreaks
	Pale leaves, weak growth	Inadequate light; or if seedlings are receiving enough light, a symptom of nitrogen deficiency	Provide stronger light. Feed with water-soluble fertilizer rich in nitrogen (nitrogen content indicated by first number in three-number fertilizer formula; e.g. *10* – 6 – 4)
	Purplish-colored, weak-looking seedlings	Phosphorus deficiency	Have soil tested, and fertilize as indicated with rock phosphate or super-phosphate; excessively acidic soil can block roots' absorption of phosphorus

PLANS AND PLANTS

PART 3

You need plants,

of course, to garden successfully, but you also need a plan. Without a plan it's almost impossible to select the right combinations of seeds, the ones that suit your requirements and those of your site. On the following pages, you'll find sample plans for two kinds of gardens Martha would never want to be without: a cutting garden and a kitchen garden. You'll also find our Plant Glossary, which gives individual profiles of more than one hundred kinds of seeds. Besides

supplying details about special care each kind of seed may require, and tips on tending the plant it produces, these profiles list Martha's favorites—the varieties of each flower (both annual and perennial), vine, herb, and vegetable she has tried and found to be the very best.

A CUTTING GARDEN

There is no greater luxury than having a house full of fresh flowers. By growing your own cutting flowers from seed, it is possible to enjoy extraordinary colors, fragrances, and shapes you will never find at the florist, or even amid the stock of potted transplants at a local nursery or garden center. And because you get to select every one of your "ingredients," the arrangements you compose with them can't help but express your personal style.

SELECTING A SITE Though a cutting garden is, by definition, a source of beauty, the first requirement for a well-planned layout is productivity, not the aesthetic appeal of the design. Seasoned gardeners usually choose to tuck this utilitarian plot in some unobtrusive part of the backyard. They know that making a cutting garden the visible centerpiece of a landscape inevitably creates a conflict: Whenever it's time to cut flowers for a bouquet, you'll be torn between your desire to fill a vase indoors and your reluctance to leave an unsightly gap in the garden.

A common tactic is to link the cutting garden to the kitchen, or vegetable, garden, another place where abundance and practicality are top priorities. (To simplify maintenance and keep out hungry deer and other pests, many gardeners enclose the two areas within a continuous fence.) In fact, both types of plantings prefer the same conditions: an open, sunny spot with fertile, well-drained soil. Six hours of unobstructed sunlight a day is ideal for most flowers used in arrangements, though by putting in shade-tolerant plants such as baby blue-eyes and scarlet sage you can have resources for cutting even in locations where daily direct sunlight does not exceed four hours.

ARRANGING THE PLANTS For the best-quality blooms, grow plants at the proper spacing (see the Plant Glossary, which begins on page 60) within rows or blocks, each devoted to a single kind of flower. Growing all of your snapdragons or mealycup sage together, for instance, makes it easier to give each type of plant the particular treatment it needs. These groupings also make it easier to locate the varieties you want when you are collecting stems for an arrangement. As a rule, allot each kind of plant a block measuring at least two feet by two and one-half feet.

Grouping plants in the garden by color is another way to simplify your flower gathering. Plant all the yellows and golds together in one area, say, and all the lavenders and mauves in another, and you'll always know where to find the exact tone you desire.

PLANTING FOR VARIETY For interesting arrangements, you'll need a variety of floral forms as well as colors. For example, consider growing tall spires such as delphiniums and rounded flowers such as African marigolds and globe amaranth, as well as airy fillers like baby's breath and feather top grass. And plan ahead, with everlastings such as strawflowers, which you can dry for winter arrangements.

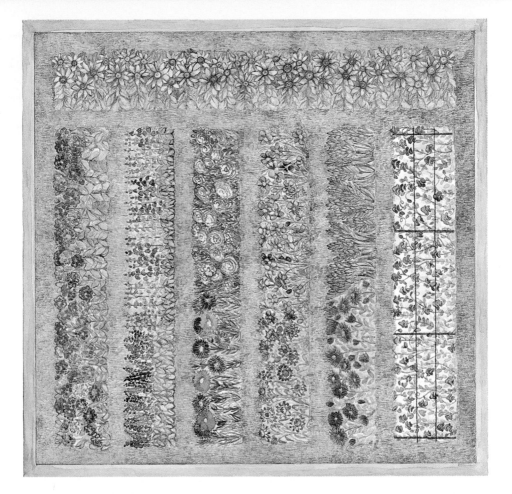

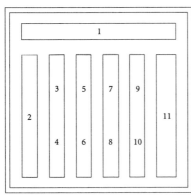

NORTH

Measuring about 20 by 20 feet, this garden supplies enough flowers to cut for two arrangements a week; from summer into fall, as well as flowers for drying.

1. SUNFLOWERS: *Smaller, pollenless 'Chianti' mixes well in arrangements*

2. ZINNIAS: *Bloom from midsummer into fall, in every color but blue; 'Envy' is chartreuse; 'Cut and Come Again' mix yields pinks, yellows, and whites*

3. SNAPDRAGONS: *Tall 'Cinderella' mix is best for cutting*

4. MEALY-CUP SAGE: *Spiky flowers in blues, violets, and whites*

5. MARIGOLDS: *For cutting, try taller African marigold (Tagetes erecta)*

6. CHINA ASTERS: *Lush, reliable bloom from summer well into fall*

7. COSMOS: *Gracefully long-stemmed; Cosmos bipinnatus has fluted flowers*

8. STRAWFLOWERS: *Old-fashioned favorites for dried arrangements*

9. COCKSCOMB: *Dramatic red or yellow plumes and fuzz; use fresh or dried*

10. CALENDULA: *Daisylike yellow to orange flowers; can be dried for potpourri; replace with a late sowing of bachelor's buttons*

11. SWEET PEAS: *Reds, blues, pinks, whites; fragrant vine; best on a trellis*

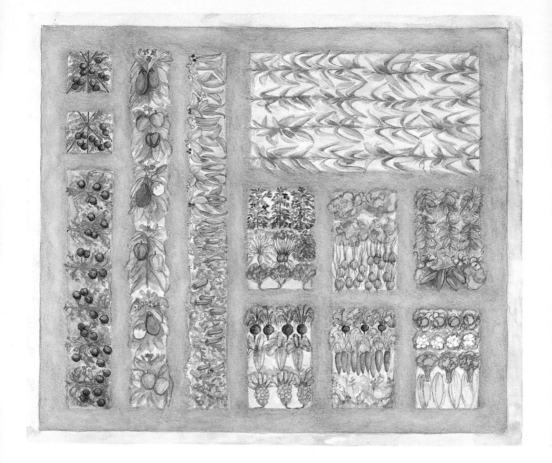

NORTH

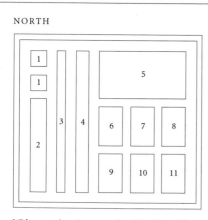

With repeated sowings as noted at right, this roughly 20 by 20 foot patch would supply a family of four with fresh vegetables from early spring into late fall.

1. CHERRY TOMATOES: *Grow on wooden tepees or metal cages with other indeterminate varieties; for a definition of "indeterminate," see page 108*

2. DETERMINATE TOMATOES: *These are the best varieties for sauce-making and canning; for a definition of "determinate," see page 108*

3. EGGPLANT *(purple and white)* and PEPPERS *(sweet and hot)*

4. PEAS *(shelling and snap) in spring;, replaced by* BUSH BEANS *in summer*

5. SWEET CORN: *For a steady supply, sow every 2 weeks*

6. CHIVES, DILL, PARSLEY, SWEET BASIL, *and other culinary herbs*

7. LETTUCE *(looseleaf for cut-and-come-again harvest), spring;* ONIONS, *summer*

8. SPINACH, *spring;* CUCUMBERS, *summer (sow one hill)*

9. BEETS, SWISS CHARD, *spring;* KALE, BRUSSELS SPROUTS, *fall*

10. RADISHES, CARROTS, *spring;* MESCLUN MIX, *fall*

11. CABBAGE *(mix small and large varieties)*, CAULIFLOWER *('Early White')* BROCCOLI, *spring;* COLLARDS, KALE, TURNIPS, *fall*

A KITCHEN GARDEN

Freshness is the most important spice for any dish of vegetables, yet true freshness is rare in the produce section of the supermarket—reason enough to sow the seeds for a vegetable and herb garden that will yield harvests from early spring through late fall.

SELECTING A SITE Six hours of full sunlight is the minimum daily requirement for most vegetables and herbs; without this ration, your tomatoes and peppers, squash, cucumbers, and corn won't bear fruit, and your sweet basil will languish. Some leafy greens, such as spinach and lettuce, will grow adequately in light shade, but even they are more prolific in full sun. Look for an open patch of ground without any overhanging branches or tall trees on the south side. Indeed, in Northern regions where sunlight is less intense—especially in areas with cloudy climates—it's best to set the garden on a gentle, south-facing slope. Angled toward the direction from which the sunlight comes, such plots receive maximum solar rays.

ORIENTING THE BEDS On a sloping site it is best to run beds across the slope, to block water runoff and reduce soil erosion. In regions where the sun is most intense, as in the Southwest, run beds from east to west; this allows each plant to lend a bit of shade to its neighbors as the sun travels across the sky. Though, as a rule, vegetables prefer full sun, some relief is beneficial in the hottest, sunniest parts of the country.

Conversely, in a Northern garden, avoid planting tall crops along the south side of a bed. In that location, stands of sweet corn or sunflowers will shade any lower-growing neighbors you have planted to their north, and so deprive them of precious sunlight.

KEEPING A SENSE OF SCALE Renting a rototiller makes it easy to carve out a huge vegetable garden, but keeping such a plantation weeded and watered can prove burdensome. Consult the chart on page 31, and plant no more than your household is likely to consume. Expand the garden only as you have the time and the need, adding one new bed at a time.

MAKING RAISED BEDS Martha prefers to grow her vegetables in raised beds, planting areas in which the soil has been built up above the level of the surrounding soil. Such beds thaw and warm more quickly in the spring, allowing earlier planting. They also provide good drainage, ensuring that excess moisture drains away before it can drown the vegetables' roots.

Raised beds may be framed with timbers (avoid railroad ties and other wood treated with preservatives, which can leech into the soil) or simply heaped up and raked level. Extend them to any length you like, but do not make them more than four feet across. You should be able to reach comfortably into the center of the bed without stepping into it, so that you can plant and weed without compressing the soil, which deprives roots of oxygen. Never step on the soil, and you won't have to redig continually. Turning the soil is not only hard work, it also reduces soil fertility.

REPLANTING AND ROTATING Vegetable gardeners should plan to replant their plots at least once a season (see pages 46-47). Chill-tolerant spring crops must be replaced by heat-tolerant ones as the summer settles in, and summer crops replaced in turn by cool-loving plants when fall arrives (see the chart on pages 49-51 for recommendations of what edibles to sow when, according to region). Draw up a plan of your beds, to scale, on graph paper and photocopy it. Then sketch in each season's plantings on a separate sheet.

Change your planting scheme not only from season to season, but also from year to year. As a rule, each vegetable has its own diseases and pests. Planting a crop in the same space year after year encourages its enemies to entrench themselves in the soil there, guaranteeing chronic pest-control problems.

BABY BLUE EYES

Nemophila menziesii

HEIGHT: 6 TO 10 INCHES; **SPACE OR THIN TO:** 6 TO 9 INCHES APART; **SUN:** LIGHT SHADE; **SOIL:** RICH, MOIST, WELL DRAINED

SOW: Direct sow—in cold-winter regions, sow in spring as soon as soil can be worked; in mild-winter regions, sow in fall. Or sow indoors in peat pots or pellets, 5 to 7 weeks before transplanting in mid-spring. Barely cover the seeds. Germinates in 7 to 14 days.

In spring, this sprawling, low-spreading plant bears dainty, cup-shaped blue-and-white or pure white flowers. It makes an ideal companion for bulbs in a cool-spring garden. In pots and window boxes, *N. menziesii* spills over the sides. Baby blue eyes is a good choice for north-facing locations and shadier areas of the cutting garden.

This California wildflower has been cultivated in England for more than a century. It is also commonly used in commercial wild-flower mixes. The Latin name *Nemophila* comes from two Greek words, *nemos* (a glade) and *phileo* (to love), because the plant prefers the shade.

GARDEN HINTS: Baby blue eyes dies back as summer's heat and humidity settle in. Watch for aphids on the foliage (for treatment, see Pests and Diseases, page 52).

BABY BLUE EYES

BABY'S BREATH

Gypsophila elegans

HEIGHT: 18 TO 24 INCHES; **SPACE OR THIN TO:** 8 TO 12 INCHES APART; **SUN:** FULL; **SOIL:** WELL DRAINED, SLIGHTLY ALKALINE (BUT PLANT WILL TOLERATE NEUTRAL PH)

SOW: Direct sow—in most regions, sow in spring; in mild-winter regions, sow in fall or early spring. Lightly cover seeds. Germinates in 10 to 15 days.

An easy-to-grow plant, native to Asia Minor, the Caucasus, and Ukraine, baby's breath flourishes in the cool weather of spring, blooming in early summer. The delicate clouds of small white-to-pink flowers borne on slender stems make a perfect foil to other, bolder flowers both in the garden and in bouquets. Beautiful fresh or dried.

GARDEN HINTS: Baby's breath has a short bloom period. To extend your display, make second and third sowings at 2- to 3-week intervals. Baby's breath is remarkably drought tolerant, once established.

MARTHA'S SELECTION: 'Covent Garden'—The long-stemmed, large, single white flowers are ideal for cutting.

'COVENT GARDEN'
BABY'S BREATH

'BLUE BOY'
BACHELOR'S BUTTON

BACHELOR'S BUTTON

Centaurea cyanus

HEIGHT: 12 TO 36 INCHES; **SPACE OR THIN TO**: 6 TO 9 INCHES APART; **SUN**: FULL; **SOIL**: WELL DRAINED

SOW: Indoors 3 to 4 weeks before last frost; transplant around the date of the last frost. Or direct sow after danger of frost is past. In mild climates, direct sow in fall. Sow seeds ¼ inch deep. Germinates in 7 to 14 days.

This easy-to-grow summer bloomer bears fluffy, thistle-like blossoms of blue, purple, yellow, white, pink, or red that measure up to 1½ inches across.

This plant is also known as cornflower, a name that refers to the fact that it was once typically found growing amid field-grain crops (collectively referred to as corn) in Europe. Other plants named for their association with grain fields are corn-cockle, corn poppy, and corn marigold.

GARDEN HINTS: *Centaurea cyanus* thrives in the cool weather and short days of spring. When started during the long days of July or August, the plants are shorter and produce fewer flowers. Unlike many annuals, bachelor's buttons seem to bloom more profusely when the plants are a little crowded, planted 6 inches apart.

MARTHA'S SELECTION: 'Blue Boy'–Light-blue 1- to 1½-inch flowers are borne on densely branched 3-foot-tall upright plants.

BELLS OF IRELAND

BELLS OF IRELAND

Moluccella laevis

HEIGHT: 24 TO 36 INCHES; **SPACE OR THIN TO:** 9 TO 12
INCHES APART; **SUN:** FULL; PARTIAL IN HOT CLIMATES;
SOIL: BALANCED PH, WELL DRAINED

SOW: Direct sow after danger of frost is past; does not transplant well. Lightly press seeds into soil—direct light needed for germination. Germinates in 25 to 35 days.

A white-veined, light-green 1-inch bell surrounds and hides each small, white flower; the blossoms are borne in spikes. Bells of Ireland is a striking garden complement to deep-purple flowers, and an intriguing cut flower when fresh, or when dried to a light tan.

Also known as shell flower, *M. laevis* originated far from the Emerald Isle, in the Causasus, Turkey, Syria, and Iraq.

GARDEN HINTS: This cool-season annual grows best where summers are not hot and humid. When cutting, beware of sharp spines hiding under flowers. For drying, cut stems before seeds ripen; if cut too late, flowers become brittle.

CALENDULA

Calendula officinalis

HEIGHT: 24 INCHES; **SPACE OR THIN TO:** 9 TO 15 INCHES
APART; **SUN:** FULL; **SOIL:** BALANCED PH, WELL DRAINED

SOW: Indoors, 3 to 4 weeks before last frost or direct sow after danger of frost is past. In frost-free regions, sow in fall. Sow seeds ¼ inch deep. Germinates in 7 to 14 days.

At home in beds or borders, or in the herb garden, calendulas bear daisylike single or double blossoms that range in diameter from ½ to 4 inches, and in color from yellow to deep orange. The marigoldlike flowers were once used to flavor soups and stews (hence their other common name, "pot marigold"); the petals can be dried for potpourri.

GARDEN HINTS: Because they have large seeds, bloom in bright colors, and are easy to grow, calendulas are perfect for a child's garden. Deadhead them regularly for more blooms. This cool-season annual is best in areas with mild summers.

MARTHA'S SELECTIONS: 'Greenheart Orange'—Bears 2-inch flowers of soft orange petals surrounding a pale-green center.

**'GREENHEART ORANGE'
CALENDULA**

CHINA ASTER

Callistephus chinensis

HEIGHT: 9 TO 12 FEET; SPACE OR THIN TO: 9 TO 12 INCHES APART; SUN: FULL; SOIL: RICH, MOIST, WELL DRAINED

SOW: Indoors 3 to 8 weeks before last spring frost; or direct sow in spring after danger of frost is past. Lightly cover seeds. Germination time can be erratic, taking anywhere from 8 to 14 days.

This annual blooms from mid to late summer, generally performing best where summers are not uncomfortably hot. Flowers may be single, double, or semidouble, in a variety of petal shapes and glorious colors.

GARDEN HINTS: Avoid planting china asters in the same place year after year, to help prevent diseases from overwintering in the soil. Deadhead regularly to lengthen the period of bloom.

MARTHA'S SELECTION: 'Giant Princess' mix—Purple, light-blue, pink, red, and yellow 3- to 4-inch flowers. Curled outer petals combine with quill-like inner ones to create a crested appearance. The long, sturdy flower stems are perfect for cutting.

'GIANT PRINCESS' MIX CHINA ASTER

COLEUS

Solenostemon scutellarioides

HEIGHT: 10 TO 12 INCHES; SPACE OR THIN TO: 12 TO 18 INCHES APART; SUN: FULL OR PARTIAL; SOIL: BALANCED PH; MOIST BUT WELL DRAINED

SOW: Indoors, 6 to 8 weeks before last frost, in plastic cell packs or in pots; transplant after all danger of frost is past. Lightly press seeds into seed-starting mix—direct light needed for germination. Keep warm and moist. Germinates in 10 to 15 days.

This plant's vivid, variegated foliage (in a spectrum of purples, reds, oranges, yellows, and greens) electrifies window boxes, other containers, and borders; coleus is also one of the best sources of color for shady gardens. Move seedlings outdoors as soon as the weather has warmed and all danger of frost is past. Coleus thrives in summer heat and humidity, lasting until fall frost.

GARDEN HINTS: To encourage bushiness, pinch back stems of young plants and remove flower buds from older ones. The flowers' color is more intense when coleus is planted in light shade.

MARTHA'S SELECTION: 'Golden Wizard'—A dwarf, rounded coleus with striking golden foliage.

'GOLDEN WIZARD' COLEUS

'SONATA' COSMOS

COSMOS

Cosmos bipinnatus, C.sulphureus

HEIGHT AND SPACING: VARY BY SPECIES; **SUN:** FULL; **SOIL:** BALANCED PH; WELL DRAINED

SOW: Direct sow when all danger of frost is past. Or sow indoors, 4 to 6 weeks before last frost; transplant after last frost. Sow seeds ¼ inch deep. Keep warm and moist. Germinates in 5 to 10 days.

Cosmos are very easy to grow, and their long stems and cheerful blooms make them excellent cut flowers.

Though this plant has its origins in Mexico, the name derives from *kosmos*, the Greek word for "beautiful."

GARDEN HINTS: For sturdier plants, set seedlings deep at transplanting time. Avoid rich soil, which promotes leaf growth at the expense of flowers. Deadhead to prolong bloom. Plant taller cultivars in an area protected from wind, and stake them.

MARTHA'S SELECTIONS: *C. bipinnatus* 'Sonata White'—Dwarf with 4-inch wide flowers. Height: 18 inches. Thin to: 18 to 24 inches apart. *C.bipinnatus* 'Sensation' mix—Satiny petals on 3-inch blooms are slightly fluted. Height: 4 to 6 feet. Thin to: 18 to 24 inches apart. *C. sulphureus* 'Bright Lights' mix—Small semi-double flowers in shades of yellow, orange, and scarlet. Height: 3 feet. Thin to 1 to 2 feet apart.

'SENSATION' MIX COSMOS

'BRIGHT LIGHTS' MIX COSMOS

FEATHERTOP GRASS

Pennisetum villosum

HEIGHT: 18 TO 24 INCHES; **SPACE OR THIN TO:** 12 TO 18 INCHES APART; **SUN:** FULL; **SOIL:** MODERATELY FERTILE, WELL DRAINED

SOW: Direct sow 6 to 8 weeks before last frost. Barely cover seeds. Germinates in 10 to 21 days.

From zone 9 southward, this grass is perennial; to the north, it must be replanted every year. Its mat of bright gray-green leaves is handsome, but the flowers that arch above the foliage in mid to late summer are the real attraction. Creamy white, the woolly 6-inch plumes add a special texture to flower arrangements when fresh cut; dried, they may be added to wintertime displays of "ever-lastings" (the term for grasses and flowers that dry easily and retain their colors for months or even years).

In Latin, *penna* means feather, *seta* means bristle, and *villosus* means shaggy. Put it all together, and "shaggy feather bristle" is an apt description of the fluffy seed heads of feathertop grass.

GARDEN HINTS: Harvest seed heads as they mature; harvest plumes in full bloom. Dry upright in small bundles in an airy, cool place.

FEATHERTOP GRASS

GLOBE AMARANTH

Gomphrena globosa

HEIGHT: 24 INCHES; **SPACE OR THIN TO:** 12 INCHES APART; **SUN:** FULL; **SOIL:** WELL DRAINED

SOW: Indoors, 3 to 4 weeks before transplanting outdoors; transplant or direct sow after all danger of frost is past and weather is warm. Sow seeds ¼ inch deep; outdoors, sow thinly and cover with ¼ inch of fine soil. Germinates erratically, in 10 to 21 days.

This old-fashioned flower, which bears ¾-inch cloverlike blossoms of white, pink, lilac, and dusty red, is mostly grown for use in dried flower arrangements and wreaths. It is beginning to gain popularity as a flower for fresh bouquets. Because it blooms for a long time, from midsummer to frost, and has a tidy shape, globe amaranth is also excellent in beds and mixed borders. Easy to grow, *G. globosa* is rarely bothered by pests and diseases, and blooms even in poor soil, heat, and drought.

GARDEN HINTS: To dry globe amaranth for winter use, harvest when flowers are completely open. Remove the leaves, bunch the blooms loosely, and hang them upside down in an airy, cool, shady place.

MARTHA'S SELECTION: A cutting mix of white, pink, and red.

GLOBE AMARANTH CUTTING MIX

IMPATIENS

Impatiens walleriana

HEIGHT: 6 TO 26 INCHES; **SPACE OR THIN TO:** 9 TO 12 INCHES APART; **SUN:** PARTIAL; **SOIL:** MOIST, RICH, WELL DRAINED

SOW: Indoors, 6 to 8 weeks before last frost; transplant after all danger of frost is past. Press seeds lightly into seed-starting mix; direct light needed for germination. Germinates in 10 days.

Impatiens needs only a few hours of sun each day to produce gorgeous mounds of flowers from spring until first frost. This plant can be used to bring color to borders, as a ground cover in shady spots, or in containers and hanging baskets. Impatiens takes its name from the Latin for "impatient," but not because there's much of a wait for its flowers to come forth. Rather, it's because the slightest touch causes ripe seed pods to burst, scattering seeds as if they were impatient to do so.

GARDEN HINTS: Impatiens are tropical hybrids and need to be kept evenly moist to continue blooming. Be vigilant watering during dry spells. Fertilize if leaves turn light green.

MARTHA'S SELECTION: Light pink hybrid—Many large rosy flowers—up to 2 inches across—on well-branched, compact plants that don't need pinching.

LIGHT PINK HYBRID
IMPATIENS

LARKSPUR

Consolida ambigua

HEIGHT: 3 TO 4 FEET; **SPACE OR THIN TO:** 12 INCHES APART; **SUN:** FULL; **SOIL:** RICH IN ORGANIC MATTER, WELL DRAINED

SOW: Direct sow—in cold-winter regions, sow in spring as soon as soil can be worked; in mild-winter regions, sow from fall to early spring. Sow seeds ¼ inch deep. Germinates in 15 to 20 days.

This fast-growing delphinium look-alike relishes cool weather, typically blooming in early summer; flowering is more prolonged in cooler, less humid climates. Depending on the cultivar, larkspurs bear small single or double flowers in brilliant shades of sky and dark blue, pink, carmine, salmon, and white; these are held aloft on tall, upright spires.

Larkspurs also make outstanding cut flowers, and the flower spikes retain their rich colors when dried. If allowed to self-sow, larkspurs often form self-sustaining colonies.

GARDEN HINT: Taller varieties may need staking or other support.

MARTHA'S SELECTION: 'Giant Imperial' mix—Produces flowers of dark and sky blue, lilac, carmine, rose, salmon, pink, and white on 3-foot-tall plants.

'GIANT IMPERIAL' MIX
LARKSPUR

LOVE-IN-A-MIST

Nigella damascena

HEIGHT: 18 INCHES; **SPACE OR THIN TO:** 6 TO 9 INCHES APART; **SUN:** FULL; **SOIL:** FERTILE, WELL DRAINED

SOW: Direct sow after danger of frost is past; this has a tap root and resents transplanting. In warm areas, sow in fall. Barely cover seeds; light needed for germination. Germinates in 10 to 15 days.

For a splash of blue at the front of a flower border, nothing has the effect of a mass of nigella. Blooming from mid to late summer, it bears sky-blue, 1 ½ -inch flowers that are followed by decorative, horned seedpods that may be dried and kept for winter arrangements. The flowers can also be cut and displayed fresh or dried. *N. damascena* loves cool climates; it will fade during hot, dry summers.

A Mediterranean native, love-in-a-mist also goes by the contradictory common name "devil-in-a-bush," referring to its horned seedpods.

GARDEN HINTS: Harvest flowers when fully open; harvest seedpods when they are green with a purplish stripe. Hang flowers or pods to dry upside down in small bundles in an airy, cool, shady place. Trimming each stem to a single seedpod will make the stalks more manageable.

LOVE-IN-A-MIST

LOVE-LIES-BLEEDING

Amaranthus caudatus

HEIGHT: 3 TO 5 FEET; **SPACE OR THIN TO:** 18 TO 24 INCHES APART; **SUN:** FULL, LOVES HEAT; **SOIL:** MODERATELY FERTILE, MOIST, WELL DRAINED

SOW: Indoors, in individual pots 2 to 3 weeks before planting outside. Transplant or direct sow after danger of frost is past and weather has warmed. Barely cover seeds; light needed for germination. Germinates in 10 to 15 days.

Love-lies-bleeding blooms from mid to late summer, bearing drooping ropelike clusters of deep-red flowers on a bold, tall stalk. May require staking. Cut for fresh or dried arrangements.

This distinctive heirloom, also known as chenille plant, tassel plant, and velvet flower, takes its botanical name *Amaranthus* from the Greek for "without wither," referring to the plant's long-lasting nature.

GARDEN HINT: Don't harvest love-lies-bleeding until the seeds have begun to set and the flowers feel firm. Cut early, they may shrivel. Remove leaves, and dry upright in tall buckets in a cool, airy place.

LOVE-LIES-BLEEDING

'QUEEN SOPHIA'
FRENCH MARIGOLD

MARIGOLD

Tagetes patula, T. tenuifolia

HEIGHT AND SPACING: VARY BY SPECIES AND CULTIVAR;
SUN: FULL; **SOIL:** ORDINARY, WELL DRAINED

SOW: Direct sow when all danger of frost is past. In cold regions, sow indoors 4 to 6 weeks before last frost date; transplant after all danger of frost is past. Sow seeds ⅛ inch deep. Germinates in 5 to 7 days.

Heat-tolerant flowers (native to Mexico and Central America, regardless of their common names) bloom through summer until first frost.

GARDEN HINT: Pinch off the growing tips of young plants to encourage branching. Flowers are edible (if not sprayed with chemicals).

MARTHA'S SELECTIONS: French marigold, *T. patula* 'Queen Sophia'—Rounded plants with 2½- to 3-inch russet flowers tipped with yellow. Ideal for edging beds or as a filler in the annual border. Height: 8 to 10 inches. Thin to: 10 to 12 inches apart. African marigold, *T. erecta* 'Snowdrift'—Tall plants, great for cutting, bear 3½-inch flowers in soft creamy white. Height: 22 inches. Thin to: 15 to 18 inches apart. Signet marigold, *T. tenuifolia* 'Tangerine Gem'—Lacy foliage with lemon-verbena fragrance. Wonderful in containers and borders; great for edging a vegetable patch. Masses of ½-inch orange flowers. Height: 10 to 24 inches. Thin to: 10 to 14 inches apart.

'SNOWDRIFT'
AFRICAN MARIGOLD

'TANGERINE GEM'
SIGNET MARIGOLD

MEALY-CUP SAGE

Salvia farinacea

HEIGHT: 18 TO 30 INCHES; **SPACE OR THIN TO:** 12 INCHES APART; **SUN:** FULL; **SOIL:** FERTILE, MOIST, WELL DRAINED

SOW: Indoors, 4 to 6 weeks before last frost; transplant or direct sow in spring after danger of frost is past. Lightly press seeds into seed-starting mix or soil—direct light needed for germination. Germinates in 14 to 21 days.

Bees, butterflies, and hummingbirds flock to the blossoms that mealy-cup sage bears through the summer and until the first fall frost. The spiky flowers are also a welcome accent in arrangements. Where frosts are infrequent (zones 8 through 11), this plant is perennial; elsewhere, it must be replanted each year. This is one of the huge number of plants in the genus Salvia, which includes sturdy shrubs and dainty dwarfs, herbs to cook with and flowers to look at, perennials, biennials, and annuals.

GARDEN HINTS: Pinch young plants to encourage bushiness. Water deeply during hot, dry spells.

MARTHA'S SELECTIONS: 'Strata'—An award winner with unusual bicolor flowers in blue and white on 18- to 24-inch plants. Excellent in beds and borders, especially when planted in drifts.

'STRATA' MEALY-CUP SAGE

MEXICAN SUNFLOWER

Tithonia rotundifolia

HEIGHT: 4 TO 6 FEET; **SPACE OR THIN TO:** 2 TO 3 FEET APART; **SUN:** FULL; **SOIL:** BALANCED PH, WELL DRAINED

SOW: Indoors in large peat pots 3 to 4 weeks before last frost; transplant anytime after last frost. Or direct sow in spring after danger of frost is past and soil has warmed. Lightly cover seed. Germinates in 7 to 14 days.

Attractive when planted in clumps of three or five. Works wonderfully at the back of a sunny border with its relatives, the sunflowers and rudbeckias, or other brightly colored flowers. Attracts bees, butterflies, and hummingbirds.

GARDEN HINT: Deadhead Mexican sunflowers regularly to encourage more flower production.

MARTHA'S SELECTION: 'Torch'—An award-winner with vivid, fiery red-orange 3-inch-wide daisylike blooms with yellowish centers. Flowers are held on swelling trumpet stems. Wonderful for cutting.

'TORCH' MEXICAN SUNFLOWER

NASTURTIUM

Tropaeolum majus

HEIGHT: 10 INCHES OR MORE; **SPACE OR THIN TO:** 12 INCHES
APART; **SUN:** FULL; **SOIL:** BALANCED PH; WELL DRAINED

SOW: Direct sow after danger of frost is past and weather has
settled; can also be sown indoors 5 weeks before transplanting outside.
Sow seeds ½ inch deep. Germinates in 9 to 14 days.

An ideal ornament for the kitchen garden, nasturtiums bloom
from summer until frost, bearing bright white, yellow, orange, pink,
or red blossoms.

All parts of the plant are edible: The blossoms are often used to garnish
salads, the peppery leaves taste like watercress, and the flower buds
may be pickled as a substitute for capers.

GARDEN HINT: In areas where summers are very hot, nasturtiums
may stop flowering until cooler weather returns.

MARTHA'S SELECTION: 'Peach Melba'—The flowers are the light
primrose-yellow of a white peach's flesh, with raspberry-red throats.
This compact, mounding cultivar is perfect for edging borders or for
planting in containers.

'PEACH MELBA'
NASTURTIUM

NICOTIANA
LANGSDORFII

NICOTIANA

Nicotiana langsdorfii, N. sylvestris

HEIGHT: VARIES BY SPECIES; **SPACE OR THIN TO:** 12 TO 16
INCHES APART; **SUN:** FULL, TOLERATES PARTIAL SHADE;
SOIL: RICH, WELL DRAINED

SOW: Indoors, 5 to 7 weeks before last frost; transplant or direct
sow after danger of frost is past. Lightly press seeds into seed-starting
mix or soil; light needed for germination. Germinates in 14 to 21 days.

Close relatives of the tobacco plant, the nicotianas belong to the same
family as potatoes, tomatoes, and petunias, and share many of the same
pests and diseases. Nicotianas bloom from midsummer until frost.

GARDEN HINT: Once they are large enough to handle, move
seedlings to individual pots, and grow in a cool location, with day
temperatures of 50 to 55 degrees and night temperatures of 40 to
45 degrees. Self-sows reliably.

MARTHA'S SELECTIONS: *N. langsdorfii*—Tall, graceful stems
hold drooping sprays of 1-inch-long, deep-apple-green bells. Their
color blends perfectly with pinks, blues, purples, yellows, and reds.
Height: 4 to 5 feet. *N. sylvestris*—Clusters of fragrant, 4-inch-
long, white tubes ending in flared stars. The stalk rises dramatically
from a low rosette of leaves. The flowers open in the early evening
and on cloudy days, and fill the night air with perfume. Height: 3 feet.

'PURPLE WAVE'
PETUNIA

PETUNIA

Petunia

HEIGHT: 4 TO 6 INCHES; **SPACE OR THIN TO:** 1 TO 3 FEET APART; **SOIL:** AVERAGE, WELL DRAINED

SOW: Indoors, 5 to 7 weeks before last frost. Press seeds lightly into seed-starting mix; light needed for germination. In areas with a long growing season, direct sow after danger of frost is past. Germinates in 10 to 14 days.

Petunias bloom profusely from summer to fall. Since the plant spreads rapidly, it works well as a ground cover. It also does well in beds and borders, and in pots and window boxes (space the spreading varieties 3 feet apart, trailing varieties 1 to 2 feet apart).

Native to tropical regions of South America, petunias are relatives of tomatoes, peppers, and eggplants.

GARDEN HINTS: Deadhead most petunia varieties to prolong flowering (but see Martha's selection, below). Watch for aphid damage (for treatment, see page 52).

MARTHA'S SELECTION: 'Purple Wave' hybrid—An All-American Award winner, this low-growing petunia spreads 3 to 5 feet to form a flowering carpet of 2- to 3-inch fluted single blooms in deep magenta with a darker center. It is also effective in hanging baskets. More tolerant of rainy weather and drought than other petunias. 'Purple Wave' does not need to be deadheaded or cut back in midsummer. Stays in bloom throughout the season.

'DOUBLE CHOICE'
SHIRLEY POPPY

'LADY BIRD' POPPY

POPPY

Papaver commutatum, P. rhoeas

HEIGHT: VARIES BY SPECIES; **SPACE OR THIN TO:** 6 TO 8
INCHES APART; **SUN:** FULL; **SOIL:** BALANCED PH, MOIST,
WELL DRAINED

SOW: Direct sow in early spring or late fall. Lightly press seed into soil or broadcast; direct light needed for germination. Difficult to transplant; not suited to sowing indoors. Germinates in 8 to 10 days.

Bright and bold, poppies make a statement like no other annual, and every flower garden should have its share. This easy-to-grow annual blooms from early to mid summer.

GARDEN HINTS: Poppy seed is very fine. To avoid overcrowding, mix the seed with fine sand before broadcasting. Cut poppies wilt quickly unless their cut ends are seared for a second or two with a flame. The heat seals in the sap, which helps prolong the flower's life.

MARTHA'S SELECTIONS: Shirley poppy, *P. rhoeas* 'Double Choice' mix—Plants are erect and well branched. Rice-papery 3-inch double flowers in subtle yet opulent shades of pink, crimsin, salmon, red, and white. Self-sows reliably. Height: 2 to 3 feet. *P. commutatum* 'Lady Bird'—Black-spotted red petals, 3 inches across, resemble the wing markings of ladybird beetles, or ladybugs. Height: 18 inches.

**DOUBLE-FLOWERED
PORTULACA MIX**

PORTULACA

Portulaca grandiflora

HEIGHT: 4 TO 6 INCHES; **SPACE OR THIN TO:** 6 TO 12 INCHES APART; **SUN:** FULL; **SOIL:** AVERAGE, WELL DRAINED

SOW: Indoors, 6 to 8 weeks before last frost; transplant or broadcast thinly outdoors after danger of frost is past. Barely cover seeds; light needed for germination. Germinates in 5 to 10 days.

Portulaca–also known as moss rose, sun plant, or eleven o'clock–originated in Brazil, Argentina, and Uruguay. It is one of the few annuals of a succulent nature. Neither a moss nor a rose, it adapted to hot, dry climates by hugging the ground and developing tiny leaves. Large yellow, pink, white, apricot, or purple flowers lure pollinators from afar. Easy to grow, it blooms from summer into fall.

GARDEN HINTS: Portulaca seed is very fine. To avoid sowing too thickly, mix with sand before broadcasting (see page 45). Seedlings are prone to damping off (see page 16). This is the best annual for difficult, dry, sunbaked spots in the garden. Flowers open in direct sunlight and close on overcast days.

MARTHA'S SELECTION: Double-flowered mix–These low-growing plants are covered in 1-inch-wide, satiny double flowers in pink, red, yellow, and white. Excellent in containers or window boxes, along paths, or in scattered patches in a bed or border.

SNAPDRAGON

Antirrhinum spp. *(various species)*

HEIGHT: 6 TO 20 INCHES; **SPACE OR THIN TO:** 12 INCHES;
SUN: FULL; **SOIL:** RICH, WELL DRAINED

SOW: Indoors 4 to 6 weeks before last frost; transplant about the time of last frost. In mild climates, direct sow in fall. Lightly press seed into seed-starting mix or soil. Germinates in 7 to 14 days.

Use dwarf snapdragons—cultivars less than 12 inches tall—for massed bedding displays and in containers; taller cultivars make excellent cut flowers and mix easily into flower borders. Colors include white, yellow, pink, red, and purple.

GARDEN HINTS: Seedlings that have been hardened off can be planted outside 2 weeks before the last frost date. Deadhead to prolong flowering. Taller cultivars require staking. Will rebloom in fall if cut back in summer.

MARTHA'S SELECTIONS: *A. majus* 'Cinderella' mix—A vibrant combination of colorful single blooms. Uniform 20-inch height makes them a good cut flower. Pinch back tops of plants when 5 to 6 inches tall to encourage branching. Early and long period of bloom. *A. majus* 'White'—Clear-white single flowers. Early and long period of bloom. Height: 20 inches.

'CINDERELLA' MIX SNAPDRAGON

'WHITE' SNAPDRAGON

STATICE MIX

STATICE

Limonium sinuatum

HEIGHT: 24 TO 30 INCHES; **SPACE OR THIN TO:** 12 TO 15 INCHES APART; **SUN:** FULL, **SOIL:** MODERATELY FERTILE, WELL DRAINED

SOW: Indoors in individual peat pots, 8 to 10 weeks before last frost. Begin with several seeds to a pot; thin to 1 per pot. Statice has a tap root and resents transplanting. Transplant after all danger of frost is past. Barely cover seeds; light needed for germination. Germinates in 10 to 14 days.

Statice, commonly seen in florists' shops, is a perennial wildflower from the Mediterranean. Plant breeders have created many more colors than appear in nature, and these are best grown in the United States as annuals. Statice blooms from midsummer until frost. It loves dry, sunny summers and is perfect in a border of mixed annuals or in a cutting garden.

GARDEN HINT: Harvest statice flowers when they are mostly open and showing color. Tie in small bundles and hang upside down to dry in an airy, cool, shady place. Flowers and grasses that dry easily and retain their colors for months or even years are called everlastings.

MARTHA'S SELECTION: Statice mix—Papery flowers are carried in clusters on the wiry stems. Cut for fresh or dried arrangements.

'TEDDY BEAR' SUNFLOWER

'CHIANTI' SUNFLOWER

'MAMMOTH RUSSIAN' SUNFLOWER

SUNFLOWER

Helianthus annuus

HEIGHT AND SPACING: VARY WIDELY BY SPECIES AND CULTIVAR; **SUN:** FULL; **SOIL:** ORDINARY, WELL DRAINED

SOW: Direct sow when danger of frost is past. Sow seeds 1 inch deep. Germination varies by type. Blooms in mid through late summer.

Grow sunflowers as towering, eye-catching focal points for the garden, for spectacular cut flowers, and for their bird-pleasing seeds.

GARDEN HINTS: Sunflowers don't transplant well, but you can start them 2 to 3 weeks before the last frost in large peat pots, and plant the pots in the garden when all danger of frost is past.

MARTHA'S SELECTIONS: 'Teddy Bear'—Compact and bushy; ideal for containers. Chrysanthemum-like double flowers have no central eye. Height: 2 to 3 feet. Space: 18 to 24 inches apart. Germinates in 7 to 10 days. 'Chianti' hybrid—Purplish stems and dramatic deep-red 3- to 4-inch flowers flecked with gold. Pollenless blooms are perfect for arrangements indoors. Height: 4 to 5 feet on a branching stem. Space: 2 to 3 feet apart. Germinates in 10 to 14 days. 'Mammoth Russian'—Classic, single-stem tall sunflower with a 12-inch or larger head with bright yellow petals and meaty, striped edible seeds. Attracts butterflies and birds. May require staking. Height: 9 to 12 feet. Space: 2 to 3 feet apart. Germinates in 10 to 14 days.

VERBENA BONARIENSIS

Verbena bonariensis

HEIGHT: 4 FEET; **SPACE OR THIN TO:** 18 INCHES APART;
SUN: FULL; **SOIL:** BALANCED PH, MOIST, WELL DRAINED

SOW: Indoors, 5 to 7 weeks before last frost; transplant or direct sow after danger of frost is past. Sow seeds 1/8 to 1/4 inch deep. Germinates in 14 to 21 days.

A stiff, upright South American native with an airy texture, this verbena bears 2-inch flower heads, dense clusters of tiny purple blossoms that seem to float in midair. It blooms through summer until the first fall frost, making it a cottage-garden favorite. Because of its airiness, *V. bonariensis* can accent a border without hiding its neighbors.

This verbena is a species with no cultivars, so all seeds labeled *V. bonariensis* will produce identical plants.

GARDEN HINTS: Lanky seedlings should be cut back hard to encourage branching. Self-sows vigorously. Verbena bonariensis makes a long-lasting cut flower. Plant in drifts or singly. Check for aphids, whitefly, and snails (see pages 52 to 53 for treatment).

**VERBENA
BONARIENSIS**

VIOLA

Viola cornuta, V. wittrockiana

HEIGHT: 6 INCHES; **SPACE OR THIN TO:** 6 TO 9 INCHES APART;
SUN: FULL SUN TO PARTIAL SHADE; **SOIL:** RICH IN ORGANIC
MATTER, MOIST, WELL DRAINED

SOW: Indoors, 7 to 9 weeks before transplanting in early spring, up to a month before the last frost date. Sow seeds 1/8 inch deep. If seedlings have been hardened off, they will tolerate light frost. Germinates in 10 to 20 days.

Approximately 500 species make up the genus *Viola*. The most familiar varieties are commonly called viola, violet, pansy (see Martha's selections, below), and Johnny-jump-up.

GARDEN HINTS: After germinating at room temperature, grow seedlings at 50 to 55 degrees for sturdy, compact growth. Dead-head regularly to encourage new blooms.

MARTHA'S SELECTIONS: *V. cornuta* 'Trimardeau' mix—A wide range of 1 1/2-inch blooms in jewel-like shades, some with pert faces. Compact, free-flowering; good for bedding, edging, planting in pots. *V. wittrockiana* 'Jolly Joker'—This All-American Award-winning pansy is a striking bicolor with 3-inch purple-and-orange flowers. Excellent for window boxes and containers; a great edging for a mixed border.

'TRIMARDEAU' PANSY

'JOLLY JOKER' PANSY

'ENVY' ZINNIA

'CUT AND COME
AGAIN' MIX ZINNIA

ZINNIA

Zinnia elegans, z. haageana

HEIGHT AND SPACING: VARY BY SPECIES AND CULTIVAR;
SUN: FULL; **SOIL:** FERTILE, WELL DRAINED

SOW: Direct sow when danger of frost is past; or start indoors 4 to 6 weeks before last frost, transplant 1 to 2 weeks after last frost. Sow ¼ inch deep. Germinates in 7 to 10 days.

Fast-growing, easy plants, zinnias are excellent for garden color or for cutting from midsummer into fall. Especially beautiful in clusters.

GARDEN HINTS: Pinch off the growing tips of plants to encourage branching; deadhead to prolong blooming.

MARTHA'S SELECTIONS: *Z. elegans* 'Envy'—Chartreuse 3- to 4-inch double flowers. Height: 2 to 3 feet. Space: 18 to 24 inches apart. *Z. elegans* 'Cut and Come Again' mix—Double flowers in mixed colors; blooms for cutting all season long. Height: 2 to 3 feet. Space: 18 to 24 inches apart. Mexican zinnia, *Z. haageana* 'Star White': Heat, drought, and mildew resistance make this compact variety nearly perfect. 1-inch flowers in profusion and blade-shaped foliage. Best at the front of a border or as a ground cover. Height: 8 to 12 inches. Space: 12 to 18 inches apart. *Z. haageana*—'Persian Carpet' mix: Old-fashioned 1½- to 2-inch single, semidouble, and double bicolor blooms on a mounding plant. Height: to 2 feet. Space: 12 to 18 inches apart.

'STAR WHITE'
MEXICAN ZINNIA

'PERSIAN CARPET' MIX
MEXICAN ZINNIA

BLACK-EYED
SUSAN VINE

BLACK-EYED SUSAN VINE

Thunbergia alata

HEIGHT: TO 6 FEET; **SPACE OR THIN TO:** 12 TO 18 INCHES APART; **SUN:** FULL; **SOIL:** MOIST, FERTILE, WELL DRAINED

SOW: Indoors, 6 to 8 weeks before last frost; transplant or direct sow after danger of frost is past. Sow seeds ¼ inch deep. Germinates in 10 to 15 days.

A handsome, easy-to-grow plant for a hanging basket, container, or window box, the black-eyed Susan vine blooms from midsummer to frost. Also called the clock vine, the tropical African native will climb a support with its twining stems or trail over a hanging basket, window box, or other container.

The 1-inch trumpet-shaped flowers of this heirloom vine (first introduced into garden cultivation in 1825) range from yellow to orange; many have deep-purple centers—the "black eyes."

Black-eyed Susan vine's flowers may help attract hummingbirds to your garden. Just like bees, these small birds, whose wings beat up to 60 times a second, help to pollinate the flowers.

GARDEN HINTS: Black-eyed Susan vine does not flower well during the summer heat, but will make up for it as the weather cools and will flower right up to frost. *T. alata* is a perennial in its native tropics; in cooler climates, container-grown specimens may be overwintered indoors.

**'HEAVENLY BLUE'
MORNING GLORY**

**'FLYING SAUCERS'
MORNING GLORY**

**'PEARLY GATES'
MORNING GLORY**

MORNING GLORY

Ipomoea tricolor

HEIGHT: 8 TO 12 FEET; **SPACE OR THIN TO:** 18 TO 24 INCHES
APART; **SUN:** FULL; **SOIL:** AVERAGE, WELL DRAINED

SOW: In cold areas, sow indoors in peat pots, 2 to 3 weeks before last frost; transplant or direct sow after danger of frost is past. Scarify (see page 17) the hard seed coats and soak seeds in hot water for several hours before sowing. Sow seeds ½ inch deep; outdoors, sow 2 to 3 inches apart. Germinates in 5 to 10 days.

Blooming from midsummer until frost, morning glories are true to their name, in that the blossoms open in the morning and close by nightfall. Attractive heart-shaped leaves.

GARDEN HINTS: Morning-glory vines climb by twining stems. Give seedlings a small bamboo stake to get them started; all morning glories twine in the same direction—clockwise.

MARTHA'S SELECTIONS: 'Heavenly Blue'—The classic intense sky-blue flower with a white throat is 3 inches across. 'Flying Saucers'—Marbled azure and clear-white funnel-shaped bloom, 4 inches across. 'Pearly Gates'—An award-winner that loves summer heat. Its opal-white flower ranges between 4 and 5 inches in diameter.

PURPLE HYACINTH BEAN

Lablab purpureus

HEIGHT: 10 TO 15 FEET; **SPACE OR THIN TO:** 12 INCHES APART;
SUN: FULL; **SOIL:** RICH, MOIST, WELL DRAINED

SOW: Indoors in peat pots, 2 to 3 weeks before last frost. Transplant (do not disturb roots) or direct sow after danger of frost is past. Soak seeds overnight in warm water. Germinates in 7 to 14 days.

Trouble-free, fast-growing vine that relishes hot weather. In mid-summer, groups of fragrant 1-inch purple sweet pea-like flowers are carried on stiff, 8- to 10-inch-long stalks. They are followed by shiny, flat 4-inch beanlike pods that, depending on the plant, may vary in color from greenish purple to purple; inside are edible beans. The dark-green leaves also have a purple tinge.

Originally from tropical Africa, *L. purpureus* is widely cultivated on the Indian subcontinent where it is a popular vegetable.

GARDEN HINTS: This vine climbs by twining its stems, and shows to advantage when grown up a trellis or a tripod of long bamboo stakes. To make a tripod, simply tie three stakes at the top with twine or raffia, and push them into the ground next to the young plant. With just a little guidance from the gardener, the vine will know exactly what to do.

PURPLE HYACINTH
BEAN

'VIOLACEA'
SNAPDRAGON VINE

SNAPDRAGON VINE

Asarina antirrhiniflora

HEIGHT: 3 TO 6 FEET; **SPACE OR THIN TO:** 12 TO 18 INCHES
APART; **SUN:** FULL; **SOIL:** WELL DRAINED, NEUTRAL
TO SLIGHTLY ALKALINE

SOW: Indoors in February; transplant when all danger of frost is past. Germinates in 10 to 15 days.

Though this slender, branching vine is not really a snapdragon, the purple or white blossoms it bears from late summer until frost are similar in appearance. Handsome 1-inch-long leaves are ivylike. Excellent for hanging baskets or other containers.

The botanical name of this plant comes from the Greek *anti*, "like," and *rhin*, "nose," and refers to the shape of the flower. It was once believed that if worn around the neck, it would prevent the wearer from being bewitched.

GARDEN HINT: Climbing snapdragon vine climbs by twining around its host. Support with wire, strings, or slender stakes; porch columns or tree trunks are too thick for the vine to grasp.

MARTHA'S SELECTION: 'Violacea'—The purple to rose-pink flowers are 1 3/4 inches long.

SCARLET RUNNER BEAN

Phaseolus coccineus

HEIGHT: 8 TO 12 FEET, **SPACE OR THIN TO:** 4 TO 6 INCHES APART; **SUN:** PARTIAL; **SOIL:** AVERAGE, WELL DRAINED,

SOW: Direct sow after last frost, up to the end of spring. Sow seeds ½ inch deep. Germinates in 7 to 14 days. Starting indoors is not recommended.

Though this twining member of the bean family is fast growing, it is reluctant to produce seedpods in very hot weather. The clusters of diminutive crimson flowers have three-part leaves and, when mature, 10- to 12-inch-long pods containing variegated purple seeds.

When first introduced to Europe from tropical America in the seventeenth century, scarlet runner beans were grown not for their tender pods, but as ornamental additions to the garden.

GARDEN HINTS: Avoid using insecticides that harm bees. These insects are essential pollinators. Use a minimum of fertilizer; too much nitrogen promotes excess foliage at the expense of flowers and pods. Each scarlet runner bean plant produces approximately 2 pounds of beans, which are edible. Harvest the pods before the beans swell—if left on the vine, mature pods inhibit additional bean production.

SCARLET RUNNER BEAN

SPANISH FLAG

Ipomoea lobata (also known as *Mina lobata*)

HEIGHT: 9 TO 18 FEET; **SPACE OR THIN TO:** 18 TO 24 INCHES APART; **SUN:** FULL; **SOIL:** MODERATE, MOIST, WELL DRAINED

SOW: Indoors, 4 to 6 weeks before last frost; transplant after all danger of frost is past; or direct sow 2 weeks after last frost. Soak seeds in warm water overnight before sowing. Sow seeds ½ inch deep; outdoors, sow 2 to 3 inches apart. Germinates in 7 to 21 days.

A fast-growing, prolific vine. By midsummer, its arching stalks hold sprays of 1-inch tubular flowers that open a rich scarlet crimson, afterwards fading through orange to pale yellow or cream. Large, heart-shaped trilobed leaves. Blooms until frost.

Despite its common name (the vine's polychrome flowers reflect the colors of the Spanish flag), *Ipomoea lobata* is actually native to Mexico and South America.

GARDEN HINTS: Spanish flag climbs by twining stems; give seedlings a narrow bamboo stake to get them started, before they tackle a trellis.

SPANISH FLAG

'SIAM QUEEN' BASIL

'GREEN RUFFLES' BASIL

'PURPLE RUFFLES' BASIL

BASIL

Ocimum basilicum

HEIGHT: 18 TO 24 INCHES; **SPACE OR THIN TO:** 18 INCHES APART; **SUN:** FULL; **SOIL:** RICH, FERTILE, WELL DRAINED

SOW: Indoors, 6 weeks before last frost. Transplant, 4 to 5 inches apart, or direct sow when weather is consistently warm. Sow seeds ⅛ inch deep. Germinates in 7 to 10 days.

A staple of cuisines from Italy to India and Thailand, basil can also supply attractive foliage for decorative plantings. It is grown as an annual.

GARDEN HINTS: Harvested stems blacken quickly in the refrigerator, but keep fresh for days if set in a glass of water on a windowsill. You can rejuvenate basil plants in midsummer as long as they haven't yet flowered—shear them back, fertilize, and water.

MARTHA'S SELECTIONS: 'Siam Queen'—The preferred basil for Vietnamese and Thai dishes. Sweet, licorice-flavored leaves and a heady aroma of clove. Forms many side branches and provides an excellent harvest. 'Green Ruffles'—Very large, attractively puckered leaves. Excellent in soups and salads, stews and sauces. 'Purple Ruffles'—Height: 16 to 20 inches. Thin: to 12 inches apart. Fluted purple foliage and pink flowers. Mild flavor, but lovely aroma when flowers are crushed. Steep leaves to flavor and color vinegar and jelly.

CATNIP

Nepeta cataria

HEIGHT: 2 TO 3 FEET; **SPACE OR THIN TO:** 12 TO 18 INCHES APART; **SUN:** FULL, AFTERNOON SHADE IN THE SOUTH; **SOIL:** WELL DRAINED, NEUTRAL

SOW: Indoors, 3 to 4 weeks before last frost, sowing seeds ¼ inch deep. Transplant seedlings into garden when danger of frost is past. Direct sow, 6 inches apart, around time of last frost. Germinates in 7 to 14 days.

With spikes of small, white flowers, light-green scalloped leaves, and square stems, catnip is a decorative plant. Hardy in zones 8 through 3.

The major component in the oil of the plant is nepetalactone, which is said to have a sedative effect on both humans and felines. Its flowering tops and leaves can be dried and steeped: Catnip tea was a common drink in England before Chinese teas became popular.

GARDEN HINT: Young plants do not seem to be as attractive to cats, but these animals will roll on and crush older specimens unless the plants are protected by a fence. To harvest catnip, cut back to 6 inches from the ground when buds form.

CATNIP

CHERVIL

Anthriscus cereifolium

HEIGHT: 12 TO 18 INCHES, **SPACE OR THIN TO:** 9 TO 12 INCHES APART, **SUN:** FULL OR PARTIAL, **SOIL:** RICH, WELL DRAINED

SOW: Direct sow as soon as the soil can be worked, and again in late summer for fall harvest. In mild climates, sow in fall for spring crop. Does not transplant well. Sow seeds ⅛ inch deep, 1 inch apart. Germinates in 14 to 28 days. Days to harvest: 42.

With its lacy, fernlike green leaves and clusters of small, white flowers, chervil is an attractively dainty plant. It is grown as an annual.

The ancient Greek name for chervil means "herb of joy." Though the herb isn't a common culinary ingredient in America, its slight anise flavor is an essential part of French sauces and the mixed-herb seasonings and garnishes known as fines herbes (because the subtle flavor is most pronounced in the fresh foliage, and quickly fades, it is best added to cooked food in the later stages of preparation). Fresh chervil is also found in many mesclun mixes—Martha loves to add it to salads.

GARDEN HINT: Chervil does best in the cool weather of spring and fall. Pinching back flower clusters encourages more leaf production. If allowed to flower, chervil tends to self-sow.

CHERVIL

DILL

Anethum graveolens

HEIGHT: 3 TO 5 FEET; **SPACE OR THIN TO:** 12 TO 18 INCHES APART; **SUN:** FULL; **SOIL:** RICH, MOIST, WELL DRAINED

SOW: Direct sow in spring and early fall. Avoid indoor sowing. Do not cover; seeds need light to germinate. Germinates in 10 to 21 days.

Like its fellow annual cilantro, this is a dual-harvest herb. The fresh leaves are chopped into salads or added to fish, egg, and vegetable dishes; the dried seeds are used to flavor pickles, salads, and breads.

Although dill is native to the Mediterranean and Black Sea regions, the name is probably based on the old Norse *dilla,* meaning "to lull to sleep." In colonial America, children were given dill seeds to chew during church services to keep them quiet, giving rise to the common name "meeting-house seed."

GARDEN HINTS: If you see a green caterpillar with black stripes eating your dill, let it be. When it later becomes a swallowtail butterfly, you'll be glad you did. Cut off flowerheads for best leaf production. Harvest leaves at any time; harvest seeds when they turn brown.

MARTHA'S SELECTION: 'Mammoth'– A tall, handsome plant with feathery foliage and tiny, bright-yellow flowers.

'MAMMOTH' DILL

FLORENCE FENNEL

FENNEL

Foeniculum vulgare, F. vulgare var. *dulce*

HEIGHT: 4 TO 5 FEET; **SPACE OR THIN TO:** 12 INCHES APART; **SUN:** FULL; **SOIL:** AVERAGE, WELL DRAINED

SOW: Indoors, 3 to 4 weeks before last frost. Harden off and transplant when danger of frost is past and weather has settled. Sow seeds ¼ inch deep, 4 to 6 inches apart. Germinates in 10 to 21 days.

Especially in the bronze-leaved forms, this plant is decorative in both the kitchen garden and the flower border. The young, sweet leaves pick up a salad or fish dish and flavor vinegar; the dried seeds are added to apple pie. Fennel is hardy in zones 9 through 5.

GARDEN HINTS: Harvest the seeds before they fall from the seedheads and scatter. Prolific fennel can rapidly become a weed.

MARTHA'S SELECTIONS: *F. vulgare* 'Purpureum'–An ornamental grown for its finely cut foliage that emerges a bright copper color and deepens to a dark bronze. Sets off light-green or variegated foliage. *F. vulgare* var. *dulce*–Known as Florence fennel, this is grown primarily for its bulblike base that can be eaten raw or cooked. It has a crunchy texture and a celery-anise flavor. Best grown where summers are moderate; it will bolt, or flower, in hot weather. Sow again in midsummer for fall harvest.

GERMAN CHAMOMILE

GERMAN CHAMOMILE

Matricaria recutita

HEIGHT: 24 TO 30 INCHES; **SPACE OR THIN TO:** 8 TO 10 INCHES APART; **SUN:** FULL; **SOIL:** AVERAGE, WELL DRAINED

SOW: Indoors, 3 to 4 weeks before the last frost. Transplant or direct sow as soon as the soil can be worked. Transplant in clumps, as seedlings are fragile and hard to handle. Sow seeds ¼ inch deep. Germinates in 10 to 15 days.

A branching plant with lax stems and delicate, shiny leaves, German chamomile has small white, aromatic, daisylike flowers. It is commonly grown as an annual.

Sometimes called sweet false chamomile, this herb is similar in taste and effect to common chamomile, *Chamaemelum nobile*. Both are said to calm nerves and cure nightmares. German chamomile's leaves and flowers can be dried to add fragrance to potpourri. The blossoms can also be used to make tea with a subtle apple-pineapple flavor. Probably the most famous cup of chamomile tea in history is the one Mother Rabbit gives Peter after he overeats in Mr. McGregor's garden (in Beatrix Potter's classic *The Tale of Peter Rabbit*).

GARDEN HINTS: Plants produce more flowers in soil that is not overly rich. German chamomile grows quickly and dies after producing seed in midsummer. A second sowing can be made after the first dies back. Cutting flower heads encourages more production.

LAVENDER

Lavandula spp. (various species)

HEIGHT AND SPACING: VARY ACCORDING TO SPECIES;
SUN: FULL; **SOIL:** WELL DRAINED, GRITTY, NEUTRAL PH

SOW: Indoors, 4 to 6 weeks before last frost. Harden off plants, then transplant into garden when danger of frost is past. Sow seeds ¼ inch deep. Germinates in 15 to 20 days.

Not only do lavender's leaves and flowers smell fresh and sweet, they possess proven antiseptic and disinfectant qualities and were at one time frequently scattered on stored clothes to help deter moths.

GARDEN HINTS: Cut off buds that form on first-year plants to encourage stronger root production. Cut flower spikes before they are fully open for drying. Hang bunches of flower spikes to dry in an airy room away from bright light.

MARTHA'S SELECTION: English lavender, *L. angustifolia* 'Lady'– English lavender is the hardiest of the lavender species, flourishing from zone 8 up through zone 5. An All-American selection, 'Lady' blooms the first year from seed and is small enough for edging borders and paths or for growing in containers. It has a sweetly pungent aroma and appealing dark-blue flowers. Height: 10-inch-tall mound with 6-inch flower spikes. Space: 12 inches apart.

'LADY' ENGLISH
LAVENDER

MINT

Mentha spp. (various species)

HEIGHT AND SPACING: VARY ACCORDING TO SPECIES;
SUN: FULL; **SOIL:** RICH, MOIST, WELL DRAINED

SOW: Indoors, 8 to 10 weeks before last frost. Harden off and transplant or direct sow after danger of frost is past. Sow seeds ¼ inch deep. Germinates in 12 to 16 days.

In ancient Greece, mint was prized as a body rub after bathing. The Romans believed that mint spurred the appetite for meat

GARDEN HINTS: All mints grow quickly. To keep them from taking over, grow them in containers sunk in the ground. Pinch the tips of the plant in spring, and prune regularly. Rejuvenate by cutting back nearly to soil level in midsummer. To harvest, clip mint to the lowest set of clean leaves; do not pick individual leaves.

MARTHA'S SELECTION: Spearmint, *M. spicata*–Of the 500 or so different mints, spearmint is generally considered the most essential for culinary use. An excellent flavoring for iced tea, peas, and carrots, this mint is also good in tabbouleh and jelly. Toothed, sharply pointed leaves emerge from squared-off reddish stems. The lavender-colored flowers grow on spikes. Hardy in zones 4 through 9. Height: 18 to 24 inches. Space: 12 to 18 inches apart.

SPEARMINT

RA CURLED
ARF PARSLEY

PARSLEY

Petroselinum crispum, P. crispum var. neapolitum

HEIGHT: 6 TO 12 INCHES; **SPACE OR THIN TO:** 6 TO 8 INCHES APART; **SUN:** FULL OR PARTIAL; **SOIL:** RICH, WELL DRAINED

SOW: Indoors in individual pots, 8 weeks before last frost; transplant into garden 2 weeks before last frost. Direct sow, 3 to 4 inches apart, 2 weeks before last frost. Soak seeds overnight before planting; sow ¼ inch deep. Germinates in 3 to 4 weeks.

Nothing looks crisper or more appetizing than fresh parsley. A sprig of the greens may be laid on a plate as a garnish, or chopped and sprinkled just before serving over salads, soup, and egg dishes.

GARDEN HINT: Direct sowing produces more-vigorous plants. Raising seedlings indoors does not save any time; in fact, since parsley has a taproot, transplanting will only set back growth. Although parsley is technically a biennial, it is grown as an annual.

MARTHA'S SELECTIONS: Extra curled dwarf parsley, *Petroselinum crispum* —This short, curly parsley is perfect in small gardens, flower borders, or containers. Bright green with frilly leaves. Not just a garnish, parsley is vitamin rich and adds flavor to eggs, carrots, potatoes, stews, and herb butters. Height: 10 to 12 inches. Italian flat-leaf parsley, *P. crispum* var. *neapolitum*—Many people prefer flat-leaf to curly-leaf parsley for cooking. It is taller and more vigorous, and has glossy, dark-green leaves and a sweeter, more robust flavor. Height: 12 to 18 inches.

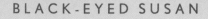

BLACK-EYED SUSAN

Rudbeckia hirta

HEIGHT: 24 TO 36 INCHES; **SPACE OR THIN TO:** 18 TO 24 INCHES APART; **SUN:** FULL; **SOIL:** WELL DRAINED

SOW: Indoors, 6 to 8 weeks before last frost. Transplant or direct sow after danger of frost is past. Lightly press seeds into soil; direct light needed for germination. Germinates in 14 to 21 days.

A Midwestern native, *Rudbeckia hirta* has spread throughout the eastern half of North America. Plants provide a mix of flowers, each with a 3- to 4-inch circle of petals ranging from bright yellow and bronze to mahogany and bicolors. The darker base surrounds a purple-black cone-shaped center; bloom continues from midsummer to fall. Leaves and stems are rough. Hardy in zones 3 through 7.

Black-eyed Susan has been the state flower of Maryland since 1918; the flower's black and gold colors also appear on the state flag.

GARDEN HINTS: Though a perennial, black-eyed Susan is often short-lived, depending on local climate and soil, and it often behaves like an annual or a biennial. To make sure it persists in your garden, leave some flowers to set seeds, so that the plant self-sows.

BLACK-EYED SUSAN

COLUMBINE

Aquilegia vulgaris

HEIGHT: 12 TO 36 INCHES; **SPACE OR THIN TO:** 10 TO 15 INCHES APART; **SUN:** LIGHT SHADE; **SOIL:** MOIST, RICH, WELL DRAINED

SOW: Indoors, 8 weeks before last frost; transplant after all danger of frost is past. Or direct sow in spring or early summer in the North, in the fall for the South. Chill seeds in refrigerator before sowing (chilling increases germination); sow ¼ inch deep. Keep at 70 to 75 degrees. Germinates in 21 to 28 days.

This European wildflower blooms in late spring to early summer, bearing blossoms of purple, violet, red, crimson, pink, or white. Hardy in zones 3 through 8.

Columbine gained the Latin name *Aquilegia,* meaning "eagle," from the shape of its base, which resembles an eagle's claw.

GARDEN HINT: In mild climates, columbines may be grown in full sun; where summers are hot, they do better in partial shade.

MARTHA'S SELECTION: 'Barlow Black'—Double, long-lasting, upward-facing flowers without the spurs typical of most columbines. This is the best columbine for cutting. Plant starts flowering the year after planting. Height: 36 inches.

'BARLOW BLACK' COLUMBINE

'PACIFIC GIANTS' MIX
DELPHINIUM

DELPHINIUM

Delphinium belladonna, D. elatum hybrids

HEIGHT AND SPACING: VARY BY SPECIES AND CULTIVAR;
SUN: FULL; **SOIL:** MOIST, SOMEWHAT ALKALINE

SOW: Indoors, 8 weeks before last frost; transplant in early spring, as much as a month before last frost. Or direct sow in spring or summer. Chill seeds in refrigerator for 2 to 4 weeks; sow ⅛ inch deep. Germination time is erratic, taking from 2 to 5 weeks.

Sovereigns of the flower border, these stately beauties bear soaring spikes of single and double blossoms in shades of pink, blue, lavender, purple, white, and bicolors from midsummer to fall. Hybrid delphiniums prefer cool, moist summers and are longest lived in zones 3 through 7. Martha likes to grow them for cutting.

GARDEN HINTS: The brittle stems should be staked. Cut back spent flower stalks to encourage reblooming, but leave a portion of the stem from which secondary flower shoots may sprout. Delphiniums need regular fertilizing.

MARTHA'S SELECTION: *D. elatum hybrids* 'Pacific Giants' mix— Flowers are usually double with darker centers. Heat tolerant. Height: 3 to 8 feet apart. Space: 1 to 3 feet apart. *D. belladonna* 'Casablanca'— Graceful branching stems hold airy, pure-white single flowers. Height: 3 to 4 feet. Space: 18 inches apart.

'CASABLANCA'
DELPHINIUM

FOXGLOVE 'EXCELSIOR'

FOXGLOVE

Digitalis purpurea

HEIGHT: 5 FEET; **SPACE OR THIN TO:** 24 INCHES APART;
SUN: FULL OR PARTIAL; **SOIL:** MOIST, WELL DRAINED

SOW: In warm regions, direct sow in fall for spring flowering; in cool areas direct sow in late spring. Lightly press seeds into soil–direct light needed for germination. Germinates in 14 to 21 days.

Foxgloves are gratification deferred: Plants started this year won't bear their purple, pink, or white flowers until late spring or summer of next year. *D. purpurea* is a biennial or short-lived perennial. Blooming plants, however, are likely to self-sow and form enduring colonies. You can tell the color of a foxglove before it blooms. Just look at the leaf stem (petiole) to see if it is flushed with a pink or purple hue; white-flowered plants lack pigment, so their leaf stems are greenish-white. Hardy in zones 4 through 8.

GARDEN HINT: Start spring plantings in a row of the cutting or vegetable garden and transplant to flower borders in fall.

MARTHA'S SELECTIONS: 'Excelsior' hybrids–Pink, cream, mauve, or white flowers, each with a speckled throat. Unlike many other foxglove hybrids, 'Excelsior' flowers encircle the spike and are held straight out instead of drooping.

GAILLARDIA

Gaillardia grandiflora

HEIGHT: 24 INCHES; **SPACE OR THIN TO:** 8 TO 15 INCHES
APART; **SUN:** FULL; **SOIL:** WELL DRAINED

SOW: Indoors in late winter in container of well-drained seed-starting mix and store in refrigerator for 6 weeks before returning to light and warmth. Transplant after danger of frost is past. Or direct sow in mid to late spring. Barely cover seeds; direct light needed for germination. Germinates in 15 to 20 days.

This native perennial blooms from early summer until frost, bearing daisylike flowers in shades of yellow, orange, and red. The flowers take their common name, blanket flower, from the similarity of their bright colors to those of Native American blankets made in the Great Plains states. Hardy in zones 3 through 10.

Gaillardia was first described by Lewis and Clark in 1806.

GARDEN HINT: Started indoors, hybrid perennial blanket flowers can bloom the first year from seed. Seedlings should be moved to a larger pot at least once to keep them from getting leggy.

MARTHA'S SELECTIONS: 'Burgundy'–These 3- to 4-inch blossoms are packed with dark, wine-red petals. Excellent as cut flowers, also impressive in mass plantings or mixed with other wildflowers.

'BURGUNDY' GAILLARDIA

HOLLYHOCK

Alcea rosea

HEIGHT: 5 TO 8 FEET; **SPACE OR THIN TO:** 18 INCHES APART;
SUN: FULL; **SOIL:** WELL DRAINED

SOW: Indoors, 2 weeks before last frost (plants will be weak if seeds are started earlier); transplant or direct sow after all danger of frost is past. Lightly press seeds into seed-starting mix or soil—direct light needed for germination. Germinates in 10 to 14 days.

Perennials treated as biennials, hollyhocks start to bloom in their second summer after sowing. They are ideal backdrops for mixed flower borders, and make excellent cut flowers if the stem end is seared with a match until black or held in boiling water for several minutes. Hardy in zones 3 through 9.

GARDEN HINTS: May require staking. Clean fallen leaves and debris from around hollyhocks in the fall to help prevent hollyhock rust, a fungal disease.

MARTHA'S SELECTION: 'Nigra'—Dramatic, almost black 3- to 4-inch blossoms with a hint of deep burgundy at the center.

'NIGRA' HOLLYHOCK

ORIENTAL POPPY

Papaver orientale

HEIGHT: 3 FEET; **SPACE OR THIN TO:** 18 TO 24 INCHES APART;
SUN: FULL; **SOIL:** RICH, WELL DRAINED

SOW: Indoors in small peat pots. Transplant in early spring 16 to 25 days after sowing, before plants become root-bound. Lightly press seeds into seed-starting mix—direct light needed for germination. Germinates in 10 to 15 days.

One of the most persistent perennials where summers are cool, poppies bloom gloriously in early summer but then fall dormant, their hairy, coarsely cut leaves dying back to the ground. To fill or hide the empty spaces, plant some neighbors that flower later, such as boltonia, perovskia, or gypsophila. Hardy in zones 4 through 9.

The Latin name, *Papaver,* means "food" or "milk," suggesting the milky fluid of the flower's pods.

GARDEN HINTS: Like most perennials, poppies don't bloom until their second summer after sowing. To use as cut flowers, sear stem ends with a match until blackened, or hold in boiling water for several minutes.

MARTHA'S SELECTION: 'Brilliant'—Fiery-red 4-inch crepelike flowers, their petals marked with a black "eye" at the base.

'BRILLIANT'
ORIENTAL POPPY

PURPLE CONEFLOWER

Echinacea purpurea

HEIGHT: 12 TO 36 INCHES; **SPACE OR THIN TO:** 18 TO 24
INCHES APART; **SUN:** FULL TO PARTIAL; **SOIL:** WELL DRAINED

SOW: Indoors in a labeled, dated pot, 6 weeks before all danger
of frost is past; place in refrigerator for 4 weeks. Transplant or direct
sow after danger of frost is past. Sow seeds ¼ inch deep. Germinates
in 15 to 20 days.

Gardeners prize this native plant's heat and drought tolerance.
Butterflies love its 3- to 4-inch blossoms with their pinkish-purple,
slightly curved petals and central brownish-bronze cone. Hardy in
zones 3 through 10.

Originally found in the Eastern and Central United States, this wildflower and its relatives have roots that were highly regarded by Native
Americans for their ability to fight infections.

GARDEN HINT: Don't deadhead; just strip away the spent petals.
The mature seedheads provide a good source of food for finches
and other birds.

PURPLE CONEFLOWER

VERONICA

Veronica spicata

HEIGHT: 12 TO 24 INCHES; **SPACE OR THIN TO:** 15 TO 18
INCHES APART; **SUN:** FULL; **SOIL:** MOIST, WELL DRAINED

SOW: Direct sow in early spring to early summer. Sow seeds ⅛
inch deep. Germinates in 7 to 21 days.

Easy to grow, this species makes a dense clump of blue or, less often,
pink or white flower spikes during its summertime season of bloom.
Hardy in zones 3 through 7.

There are many theories about the origin of the name "veronica." While
the plant may simply be named after Saint Veronica, some say the
name is derived from the Arabic *viroo nikoo* (beautiful remembrance)
or from the Greek words *phero* (I bring) and *nike* (victory), alluding
to the plant's supposed herbal benefits.

GARDEN HINTS: Divide in the spring every third year. Cut back the
spent flower stalks to encourage flowers and a more compact growth.

MARTHA'S SELECTION: 'Sightseeing' mix—Tall spikes in white and
pink as well as blue that are unusually uniform in both height and
the timing of the flowers' opening. Vigorous growers that perform well
in the garden and provide outstanding color in the front or middle
of a border. Striking as cut flowers.

'SIGHTSEEING' MIX
VERONICA

**'COLORADO' MIX
YARROW**

YARROW

Achillea millefolium

HEIGHT: 24 TO 30 INCHES, **SPACE OR THIN TO:** 18 TO 24 INCHES APART, **SUN:** FULL, **SOIL:** AVERAGE, WELL DRAINED

SOW: Indoors, two months before last frost. Lightly cover seeds with seed-starting mix; direct light needed for germination. Transplant to larger pots, then outdoors in mid spring. Germinates in 10 to 21 days.

Lacy foliage, long-lasting flowers, and an extraordinary tolerance for heat and drought make this summer-blooming perennial a garden standby. Hardy in zones 3 through 10.

The botanical name for yarrow, *Achillea,* honors the mythical Greek warrior Achilles, who was said to have used this plant to treat his wounded soldiers. These alleged medicinal properties are also the source of common names for yarrow, including "nosebleed plant" and "soldier's woundwort."

GARDEN HINT: Yarrow grows too tall and lanky if fertilized or cultivated in rich soil. After plants are established, they must be divided every two to three years to keep them vigorous.

MARTHA'S SELECTION: 'Colorado' mix— The soft colors of the desert are seen in this selection: red, russet, yellow, apricot, pink, and beige. The beautiful ferny foliage and large, 2- to 3-inch flat-topped flower heads make casual bouquets, either fresh or dried.

'PURPLE QUEEN'
BUSH BEAN

'BLUE LAKE 274'
BUSH BEAN

BEAN

Phaseolus vulgaris

SPACE OR THIN TO: 6 TO 8 INCHES APART; **SUN:** FULL;
SOIL: RICH IN ORGANIC MATTER, FERTILE, WELL DRAINED

SOW: Direct sow 2 weeks after danger of frost is past and soil has warmed. For higher yield, treat seeds with legume inoculant (available at garden centers; follow package directions) before sowing. Sow 1 inch deep every 2 to 3 inches in rows 3 to 4 feet apart. Beans resent transplanting. Germinates in 7 to 14 days.

Snap beans, also called green or string beans, are eaten whole while still immature. Shell, or horticultural, beans are removed from the pod and eaten when fully formed but still soft. Dry, or field, beans are left on the plant until the beans rattle in their pods.

GARDEN HINTS: Rotate plantings to help prevent damage from diseases or insects that overwinter in soil. Do not plant beans in the same garden spot for 3 to 4 years.

MARTHA'S SELECTIONS: 'BB Pole Wax' pole bean—Greenish-yellow bean with straight, oval pods and creamy-white seeds. Size: 5 to 7 inches; days to harvest: 68. 'Purple Queen' bush bean—Slender pods are purple when raw, green when cooked. Size: 5 to 6 inches; days to harvest: 55. 'Blue Lake 274' bush bean—Plump, tender; high yielding over a long season. Size: 5 to 6 inches; days to harvest: 58.

BEET

Beta ssp. *vulgaris*

SPACE OR THIN TO: 4 TO 6 INCHES APART; **SUN:** FULL;
SOIL: RICH, NEUTRAL PH, WELL DRAINED

SOW: Direct sow 2 to 3 weeks before last frost. In zones 8 through 10, grow as a winter or spring crop. Sow seeds ½ inch deep, every 2 to 3 inches in rows 18 to 24 inches apart. Germinates in 10 to 14 days.

A planting of beets yields two harvests: sweet, red (or, in a few cultivars, white or golden) roots, but also tangy greens for steaming or boiling. Both roots and greens are best when picked young.

GARDEN HINTS: Beets are heavy feeders; be sure to work in plenty of compost before you plant them. For root crops, soil should be loose and rock-free to a depth of 6 to 9 inches. Since crowded beets will not develop large roots, be aggressive with your thinning efforts. Thin by cutting leaves away, not by pulling the root from the ground.

MARTHA'S SELECTIONS: 'Detroit Dark Red'—An heirloom. Roots are fine textured, deep red, sweet, and tender. Glossy, maroon-tinged tops. Perfect for serving cold or hot. Size of roots: 3-inch diameter; days to harvest: 60. 'Chiogga'—Heirloom Italian beet. Flesh has bull's-eye rings. Roots and leaves both have mild flavor. Size of roots: 3-inch diameter; days to harvest: 50.

'CHIOGGA' BEET

'DETROIT DARK RED' BEET

BLACK-EYED PEA

Vigna unguiculata

SPACE OR THIN TO: 6 INCHES APART; **SUN:** FULL;
SOIL: RICH, FERTILE, WELL DRAINED

SOW: Direct sow after danger of frost is past. Treat seeds with legume inoculant (available at most garden centers; follow package directions) before sowing. Sow seeds 1 inch deep, every 3 inches in rows 2 to 3 feet apart. Germinates in 10 to 14 days.

Despite its name, this plant is actually a member of the shell bean family. You can pick the pods while young and eat them like snap beans, or leave them on the plant until they change color, then shell and cook the fresh "peas"; at season's end, pick the remaining pods and dry them before shelling out the dried peas inside.

GARDEN HINT: Never cultivate, harvest, or even brush against your bean plants when their foliage is wet. Rust diseases and blight are spread more easily among wet plants.

MARTHA'S SELECTION: 'California Black-Eyed No. 5'—Heavy yields of long pods with large seeds that can be eaten fresh at the green shell stage or left to dry on the vine. Resistant to wilt disease and nematodes. Length of pods: 8 inches; days to harvest: 75.

'CALIFORNIA BLACK-EYED NO.5' BLACK-EYED PEA

BROCCOLI

Brassica oleracea

SPACE OR THIN TO: 4 TO 6 INCHES APART; **SUN:** FULL,
SOIL: RICH, MOIST, WELL DRAINED, SLIGHTLY ALKALINE

SOW: Indoors in individual peat pots, about 6 weeks before last frost;
transplant 3 to 4 weeks later. For fall crop, direct sow 85 to 100 days
before first frost. Sow seeds ¼ to ½ inch deep; outdoors, sow 1 seed
every 3 to 6 inches in rows 12 to 18 inches apart. Germinates in 10 days.

Broccoli loves cool, moist weather, and so makes an outstanding
fall crop in most regions. Harvest heads before buds start to open
into flowers; afterward, smaller but equally delicious florets will
emerge along the stem.

GARDEN HINTS: Mulch around plants to keep soil cool and moist.
Don't grow broccoli in the same part of the garden in which another
Brassica plant was grown last year; this will avoid diseases that might
overwinter in the soil.

MARTHA'S SELECTION: 'Green Goliath'–Large blue-green heads
mature for cutting over a three-week period, providing longer harvest;
main cutting followed by many side shoots. Good for a spring or fall
crop. Extra large central head; days to harvest: 55 to 70.

'GREEN GOLIATH'
BROCCOLI

BRUSSELS SPROUT

Brassica oleracea

SPACE OR THIN TO: EVERY 2 FEET IN ROWS 3 TO 4 FEET APART,
SUN: FULL, **SOIL:** RICH, MOIST, WELL DRAINED

SOW: Indoors, 5 to 7 weeks before transplanting. Transplant 3 to 4
weeks before last frost in the North, or 90 to 100 days before first frost
in the South. Sow seeds ¼ inch deep. Germinates in 7 to 10 days.

Though technically a biennial, brussels sprout is grown as an annual
(its buds are inedible in the plant's second year). Harvest the little
cabbagelike buds from the bottom of the stalk up, through fall and into
winter–a frost will make them sweeter.

Closely related to broccoli, cauliflower, and cabbage (fellow members
of the genus Brassica), brussels sprouts are actually a form of Flanders
kale developed about 1785.

GARDEN HINT: Add 2 inches of mulch around the root zone of 10-
to 12-inch-tall plants to keep roots cool.

MARTHA'S SELECTION: 'Long Island Improved'–Also known as
'Catskill,' this brussels sprout is a widely adapted cultivar. Excellent flavor, heavy yields, and hardiness keep it a favorite. Days to harvest: 105.

'LONG ISLAND IMPROVED'
BRUSSELS SPROUT

CABBAGE

Brassica oleracea

SPACE OR THIN TO: 15 TO 18 INCHES APART; **SUN:** FULL;
SOIL: RICH IN ORGANIC MATTER, MOIST, WELL DRAINED

SOW: Indoors, 5 to 7 weeks before transplanting. Transplant 2 to 3 weeks before last frost. For a fall crop, direct sow in midsummer. In frost-free areas, direct sow in early fall. Sow seeds ½ inch deep; outdoors, sow 1 seed every 8 to 10 inches in rows 24 to 30 inches apart. Germinates in 10 to 14 days.

Cabbages vary dramatically not only in the color of the head—red or green—but also in the size; some cultivars make compact 1-pound miniheads, while others can reach a weight of 6 pounds. Choose a cultivar that suits your family's appetite.

GARDEN HINTS: The best cabbages result from stress-free growth. Healthy transplants that get regular, even watering and plenty of compost dug in before planting ensure a plentiful harvest. A floating row cover (see page 44) protects vulnerable young transplants from flea beetles and other insects; remove cover when hot weather sets in.

MARTHA'S SELECTION: 'Salad Delight'—One of the best red cabbages. Has an early harvest, with heads maturing over several weeks. Excellent fresh or lightly steamed. Size: 3 pounds; days to harvest: 50.

**'SALAD DELIGHT'
CABBAGE**

CANTALOUPE

Cucumis melo

SPACE OR THIN TO: 3 PLANTS PER HILL; OR IN ROWS, 18 TO 24
INCHES APART; **SUN:** FULL; **SOIL:** RICH, LIGHT, WELL DRAINED

SOW: Indoors in peat pots, 3 to 4 weeks before transplanting. Transplant after danger of frost is past and soil has warmed. In warm areas, direct sow 2 weeks after danger of frost is past. Sow seeds ½ inch deep; outdoors, sow 6 seeds per hill in hills 4 to 6 feet apart, or 1 seed every 12 inches in rows 4 feet apart. Germinates in 5 to 7 days.

Homegrown cantaloupes, ripened on the vine and eaten right after picking, have a sweet, perfumed perfection no store-bought melon can match. Melons need warm weather to sweeten. Summer is their prime season—just when we want them the most.

GARDEN HINTS: In cool areas, use a floating row cover to keep young plants warm. Remove the cover when flowers appear, so insects can pollinate the plants. Most melons are ripe when the gray skin changes to buff yellow and pressure at the base of stem causes the fruit to separate from the vine.

MARTHA'S SELECTION: 'Ambrosia' hybrid—Mouthwatering peach-colored flesh that's juicy, firm, and exceptionally sweet. Uniform, slightly oval melons on a productive, vigorous vine that resists powdery mildew. Size of fruits: up to 5 pounds; days to harvest: 86.

**'AMBROSIA' HYBRID
CANTALOUPE**

'SHORT 'N SWEET'
CARROT

CARROT

Daucus carota

SPACE OR THIN TO: 2 TO 3 INCHES APART; **SUN:** FULL;
SOIL: LIGHT, WELL DRAINED, AMENDED WITH COMPOST

SOW: Direct sow, beginning 1 to 2 weeks before the last spring frost (carrots do not like to be transplanted). Soak seeds for 6 hours before sowing. Sow seeds ¼ inch deep, 3 seeds to the inch in rows 12 inches apart. Germination is variable, taking as long as 14 days.

GARDEN HINTS: Soil should be loose, rich, and rock free to a depth of 6 to 9 inches for well-grown, full-size carrots. Wait for a couple of cold snaps before fall harvests, as the cold weather makes many carrots sweeter. Carrots like moderate to cool temperatures best. In warmer regions, they can be sown from fall to early spring for winter harvest. Once plants have been thinned, mound loose soil to cover the shoulders of the carrots that remain, to keep them from turning green and bitter.

MARTHA'S SELECTIONS: 'Short 'n Sweet'—Good performer in poor soils. Sweet and bright-orange right to the center. Size: 4 inches; days to harvest: 68. 'Burpee A #1' hybrid—More flavor, more sugar, more vitamin A than other carrots. Large but tender and juicy. Flavorful, good for eating fresh, cooking, or juicing. Size: 10 to 12 inches; days to harvest: 70. 'Thumbelina'—Small, round; matures early. Great for canning, freezing. Size: 1 to 1½ inches across; days to harvest: 60 to 70.

'THUMBELINA'
CARROT

'BURPEE A #1' HYBRID
CARROT

'EARLY WHITE'
HYBRID CAULIFLOWER

CAULIFLOWER

Brassica oleracea

SPACE OR THIN TO: 18 INCHES APART; **SUN:** FULL; IN AREAS
WITH HOT SUMMERS, PARTIAL SHADE; **SOIL:** RICH IN ORGANIC
MATTER, MOIST, WELL DRAINED

SOW: Indoors in peat pots or pellets 4 weeks before last frost; transplant after danger of frost is past. For fall crop, direct sow just after last frost. Sow seeds ¼ inch deep; outdoors, place two seeds every 18 inches in rows 3 feet apart. Germinates in 5 to 7 days at 70 degrees; 2 to 3 weeks in cool soil.

To produce heads of good quality, cauliflowers need cool weather and consistently moist soil; mulching the seedlings is the best insurance. Anything that checks the seedlings' growth is likely to stunt them and cause them to bear undersized heads.

GARDEN HINTS: When transplanting cauliflower, bury the seedlings almost to the lowest set of leaves. Begin "blanching," or whitening, heads when they are egg-sized; gather upper leaves around head and gently tie with twine to ensure whiteness and mild flavor.

MARTHA'S SELECTIONS: 'Early White' Hybrid—An early and very tasty cauliflower with a single, large, pure-white head that stays solid and firm. Excellent for freezing. Size: 9 inches; days to harvest: 55.

CUCUMBER

Cucumis sativus

HEIGHT: 8 INCHES; **SPACE OR THIN TO:** 18 INCHES IF TRELLISED; OR IN HILLS, EVERY 3 FEET IN ROWS 3 FEET APART, 2 PLANTS PER HILL; **SUN:** FULL; **SOIL:** RICH, FERTILE, WELL DRAINED

SOW: Indoors, 2 to 3 weeks before last frost; transplant after all danger of frost is past and soil has warmed. Or direct sow 7 to 10 days after last frost. Sow seeds ½ to 1 inch deep. Germinates in 7 to 14 days.

An easy-to-grow and rewarding crop. A single, well-tended plant can yield 30 to 40 pounds of cucumbers.

GARDEN HINTS: A floating row cover protects vulnerable young plants from cucumber beetles and unexpected cool weather. Remove row covers when flowers appear so bees can pollinate the plants.

MARTHA'S SELECTIONS: 'Burpee Pickler' pickling cucumber— An early maturer with a heavy yield of medium-green knobby fruit. Offers a long harvest period and tolerance of cucumber mosaic virus. Size: harvestable at any size; days to harvest: 53. 'Burpee Hybrid II' slicing cucumber—A vigorous grower with an early, heavy yield. Its straight fruits are best harvested when about 8 inches long. Resistant to cucumber mosaic virus and downy mildew. Size of fruits: 8 inches or more; days to harvest: 55.

'BURPEE PICKLER'
PICKLING CUCUMBER

'BURPEE HYBRID II'
SLICING CUCUMBER

'BLACK BEAUTY' EGGPLANT

'WHITE EGG' EGGPLANT

'ROSA BIANCA' EGGPLANT

EGGPLANT

Solanum melongena

SPACE OR THIN TO: EVERY 18 TO 24 INCHES IN ROWS 3 TO 4 FEET APART; **SUN:** FULL; **SOIL:** RICH, FERTILE, WELL DRAINED

SOW: Indoors, 6 weeks before last frost. Move as often as twice to larger pots to avoid root crowding, ending up in 4-inch pots. Set outdoors 2 weeks after last frost. Transplant after all danger of frost is past and soil has warmed. Sow seeds ¼ to ½ inch deep. Germinates in 7 to 10 days.

A staple in Italian, Greek, Middle Eastern, and many Asian cuisines, eggplant makes a tasty, healthy substitute for meat in vegetarian dishes.

GARDEN HINT: A floating row cover protects vulnerable young plants from insects and unexpected cool weather. Remove the cover when the plants are well established, about 1 foot high.

MARTHA'S SELECTIONS: 'Black Beauty'—Deep purple; matures earlier than other large-fruited varieties. Size of fruits: 7 inches long, 5 inches in diameter; days to harvest: 75. 'Rosa Bianca'—Italian heirloom with creamy consistency and delicate flavor. Oval fruits are a delicate white with rosy-lavender blushes. Size: 4 to 6 inches long, 3 to 4 inches in diameter; days to harvest: 80. 'White Egg'—The size of hen's eggs. A good choice for growing in a container. Space plants 18 inches apart in rows 2 to 3 feet apart. Days to harvest: 75.

LETTUCE

Latuca sativa

SPACE OR THIN TO: 6 TO 8 INCHES APART FOR CUT-AND-COME-AGAIN, 10 TO 12 INCHES FOR HEADING TYPES; **SUN:** FULL OR PARTIAL; **SOIL:** RICH, FERTILE, MOIST BUT WELL DRAINED

SOW: Indoors, 3 to 4 weeks before hardening off and transplanting. Or direct sow as soon as soil can be worked. Lightly press seeds into seed-starting mix or soil. Outdoors, sow 1 seed every 4 to 5 inches in rows 15 to 18 inches apart. Germinates in 4 to 6 days.

Looseleaf is the quickest type to grow and is best for cut-and-come-again harvesting. Butterhead, or Bibb, forms relaxed heads of soft leaves. Romaine, or cos, grows upright heads of thick, long leaves with crunchy midribs. Crisphead has tight, round heads of crispy leaves.

GARDEN HINT: For cut-and-come again harvesting, picking just the outside leaves yields more lettuce more regularly than cutting the whole plant to an inch above the soil and waiting for it to regrow.

MARTHA'S SELECTIONS: 'Royal Oak Leaf' looseleaf—Darker green, larger, and fancier than other oak-leaf types. Lobed leaves with a thick, juicy midrib. Makes a large rosette or can be harvested again and again. Days to harvest: 50. 'Four Seasons' butterhead—Burgundy outer leaves. Compact, tender 7-inch heads. Days to harvest: 54.

'ROYAL OAK LEAF' LOOSELEAF LETTUCE

'FOUR SEASONS' BUTTERHEAD LETTUCE

ONION

Allium cepa

SPACE OR THIN TO: 2 TO 3 INCHES APART; **SUN:** FULL;
SOIL: RICH IN ORGANIC MATTER, MOIST, WELL DRAINED

SOW: Direct sow 2 to 3 weeks before last frost. Soak seeds for 1 day; sow ½ inch deep every ½ to 1 inch in rows 12 to 18 inches apart. Germinates in 10 to 14 days.

Onions are classified as long-day or short-day cultivars. The long days of a northern summer promote bulb formation in long-day onions, best suited to spring planting in zone 7 and north. Short-day onions begin forming bulbs when days are shorter, and are the proper type for Southern gardens where days never get as long. Bunching, or green, onions (also called scallions) may be grown as annuals in the North or perennials (and periodically divided and replanted) in the South.

GARDEN HINTS: Onions germinate slowly in cool soil. Bunching onions can be planted thickly and pulled when quite young.

MARTHA'S SELECTIONS: 'Red Delicious'—A long-day Spanish type with bright-red skin over sweet, pinkish-white flesh. Size: large bulbs, days to harvest: 112. 'Evergreen Long White Bunching' scallion—Tender and mild, with a slightly pungent taste. Days to harvest: 65.

'RED DELICIOUS' SPANISH ONION

**'MAESTRO'
SHELLING PEA**

**'SUGAR SNAP'
SNAP PEA**

PEA

Pisum sativum, P. var. *macrocarpon*

SUN: FULL; **SOIL:** LIGHT, WELL DRAINED

SOW: Direct sow as soon as soil can be worked, 4 to 6 weeks before last frost. Treat seeds with legume inoculant (available at garden centers; follow package directions) before sowing. Sow seeds 1 inch deep, every 2 to 3 inches in rows 18 to 24 inches apart (for sugar-snap peas, space rows 30 to 36 inches apart). Germinates in 7 to 10 days.

Although separating the edible seeds from the inedible pods of shelling peas *(P. sativum)* is a lot of work, the reward is a spring delicacy. Edible-podded peas *(P. sativum* var. *macrocarpon)* such as snap peas and snow peas need no shelling, and in many cases can be eaten raw.

GARDEN HINTS: For a fall crop, find the planting date by counting back the number of days to harvest from the first expected frost, and add 2 weeks to offset cool weather. Once the plants are growing well, add 4 inches of hay mulch to extend harvest.

MARTHA'S SELECTIONS: *P. sativum* 'Maestro' shelling pea Abundant crops; sweet. Size: 26-inch vines; days to harvest: 61. *P. sativum* var. *macrocarpon* 'Sugar Snap' snap pea—Harvest edible pods when young. Trellising may increase yield. Size: 5-foot vines; days to harvest: 62. *P. sativum* var. *macrocarpon* 'Oregon Sugar Pod' snow pea—Delicious raw or stir-fried. Size: 2-foot vines; days to harvest: 68.

**'OREGON SUGARPOD'
SNOW PEA**

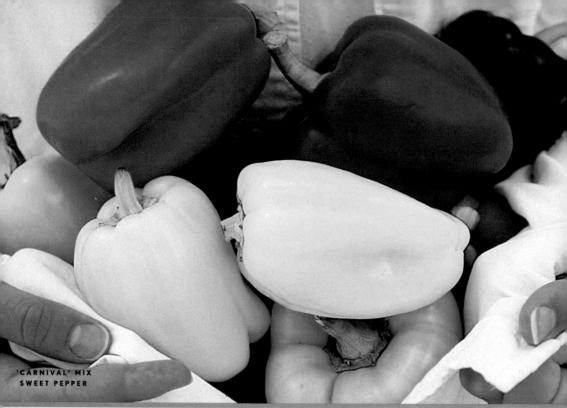

'CARNIVAL' MIX
SWEET PEPPER

PEPPER

Capsicum annuum

SPACE OR THIN TO: EVERY 18 TO 24 INCHES IN ROWS 2 TO 3 FEET APART, **SUN:** FULL, **SOIL:** FERTILE, WELL DRAINED

SOW: Indoors, 8 to 10 weeks before last frost. Seeds germinate best at 75 to 80 degrees. Transplant 2 weeks after last frost. Sow seeds ¼ to ½ inch deep. Germinates in 7 to 10 days.

Today peppers are commonly grown as annuals, but the wild ancestors of our garden cultivars were perennial shrubs.

GARDEN HINT: Don't plant outside until nighttime temperatures remain above 55 degrees. After transplanting, remove the first blossoms before the fruit sets. This encourages the plant to establish a healthy root system before it has to support fruit.

MARTHA'S SELECTIONS: 'Carnival' mix sweet peppers—Blend of five peppers: Most start green, then mature to orange, red, purple, or ivory. Size of fruits varies; days to harvest: 70 to 80. 'Cayenne Large Red Thick' hot pepper—Prolific 2- to 3-foot bushy plants. Fruits are often twisted; dry easily for winter wreaths. Size of fruits: 5 inches long, ½ inch thick; days to harvest: 75. 'Jalapeño M' hot pepper—Medium-hot; key ingredient in Mexican and Southwestern dishes. Green fruits mature to red; can be used either green or red. Good roasted, fried, pickled, or fresh. Size of fruits: 2 to 3 inches long; days to harvest: 80.

'JALAPEÑO M'
HOT PEPPER

'CAYENNE LARGE RED THICK'
HOT PEPPER

'BABY BOO'
PUMPKIN

'BIG MAX'
PUMPKIN

'ROUGE VIF D'ETAMPES'
PUMPKIN

'LUMINA'
PUMPKIN

PUMPKIN

Cucurbita pepo, C. maxima

SPACE OR THIN TO: 1 TO 2 PLANTS PER HILL, OR 2 FEET APART (3 FEET FOR VERY LARGE PUMPKINS);
SUN: FULL; **SOIL:** RICH, FERTILE, WELL DRAINED

SOW: Indoors in individual pots, 3 weeks before transplanting. Transplant after last frost. Or direct sow 2 to 3 weeks after last frost. Sow seeds 1 inch deep; outdoors, sow 5 to 6 seeds per hill in hills spaced 3 feet apart, or sow 1 seed every 12 inches (18 inches for very large pumpkins) in rows 8 feet apart. Germinates in 7 to 10 days.

Today we think of pumpkins as Halloween decorations, but our ancestors valued them for their squashlike flesh and edible seeds. Few crops are easier to grow or more reliable.

GARDEN HINTS: Pumpkins should be allowed to ripen fully on the vine. Water frequently and mulch with newspaper or grass clippings to keep soil moist. Water less frequently as pumpkins begin to ripen and the rind color dulls. Less water makes pumpkins sweeter.

MARTHA'S SELECTIONS: *C. pepo* 'Baby Boo'– Miniature; white skin and flesh; can be grown on a trellis. Bake and serve whole. Size: 3 inches across; days to harvest: 90 to 95. *C. maxima* 'Big Max'–Giant; orange; perfect for big jack-o'-lanterns. Size: 75 pounds; days to harvest: 115. *C. maxima* 'Rouge vif d'Etampes'–Heirloom imported from France in the 1880s. Custardlike flesh good for pies or soup. Size: 10 to 15 pounds; days to harvest: 110. *C. pepo* 'Lumina'–White skin; orange flesh used for pies or breads. Size: 10 to 12 pounds; days to harvest: 90 to 100.

'FRENCH BREAKFAST' RADISH

'WHITE ICICLE' RADISH

RADISH

Raphanus sativus

SPACE OR THIN TO: 2 TO 3 INCHES APART; **SUN:** FULL;
SOIL: LIGHT, WELL DRAINED, HEAVILY AMENDED WITH COMPOST

SOW: Direct sow spring radishes 3 to 4 weeks before last frost, and again in late summer or fall for harvesting close to first frost. Sow winter radishes in late summer or fall so they will mature by first frost. Sow seeds ½ inch deep, every ½ to 1 inch in rows 9 to 12 inches apart. Germinates in 3 to 5 days.

Spring radishes can furnish pickings within 3 or 4 weeks of planting. Winter radishes are slower to mature but make large crisp roots that, if mulched with several inches of straw, continue to sweeten in the ground after fall frosts have cut down the leafy upper growth.

GARDEN HINTS: Soil should be loose and rock free to a depth of at least 6 to 9 inches for well-grown, well-shaped root vegetables. An even supply of moisture prevents cracking.

MARTHA'S SELECTIONS: 'French Breakfast'—An heirloom spring variety. Crisp and pungent when young. Does better than other radishes in hot, dry climates. Size: 1¾ inches; days to harvest: 23. 'White Icicle'—Also an heirloom. Long, white root with crisp flesh and a mildly pungent taste. Firm but tender. Size: up to 5 inches; days to harvest: 30.

SOYBEAN

Glycine max

SPACE OR THIN TO: 6 TO 7 INCHES APART; **SUN:** FULL;
SOIL: RICH, FERTILE, WELL DRAINED

SOW: Direct sow 2 weeks after danger of frost is past and soil has warmed. Beans resent transplanting. Treat seeds with legume inoculant (available at garden centers; follow package directions) before sowing. Sow seeds 1 inch deep, every 2 inches in rows 20 to 30 inches apart. Germinates in 7 to 10 days.

Harvest soybeans when bright-green pods start to yellow. Boil pods for a few minutes until they begin to split, cool in cold water, and shell beans for cooking. For long storage, let pods dry on the vine before shelling.

GARDEN HINTS: Bean seeds can rot in cold, wet soil, and seedlings are very frost-tender. You will have stronger plants and better harvests if you wait until the soil has warmed before planting.

MARTHA'S SELECTION: 'Envy'—This early-bearing green soybean is a favorite where the growing season is short, and it can be a high-protein substitute for limas. Eaten fresh or dried, it has a tender but firm texture and a buttery flavor. Days to harvest: 75.

'ENVY' SOYBEAN

SPINACH

Spinacia oleracea

SPACE OR THIN TO: 5 TO 6 INCHES APART; **SUN:** FULL, OR
LIGHT SHADE; **SOIL:** AVERAGE

SOW: Direct sow in early spring or late summer. In warm regions, sow
from fall to early spring. Sow seeds ½ inch deep every 3 to 6 inches
in rows 18 to 24 inches apart. Germinates in 7 to 21 days.

A cool-weather crop, spinach grows best in spring or fall in most
regions of the United States, though it may be grown as a winter crop
in zones 9 and 10.

Originally an Asian green, spinach was first cultivated in Persia and
brought back to Europe during the Crusades.

GARDEN HINTS: To increase the yield, fertilize when the seedlings
emerge. Use thinnings as salad greens.

MARTHA'S SELECTION: 'Teton'—Its tasty dark-green leaves are
smooth and uniformly shaped, ranging from round to oblong. Grows
upright and is very slow to bolt, or flower. Days to harvest: 47-52.

'TETON'
SPINACH

SWEET CORN

Zea mays

SPACE OR THIN TO: 12 INCHES APART; **SUN:** FULL;
SOIL: FERTILE, WELL DRAINED

SOW: Direct sow when danger of frost is past and soil has warmed.
Sow seeds 1 inch deep, every 3 to 4 inches in rows 3 to 4 feet apart; or for
better pollination, plant in 4- by-4-foot blocks. Germinates in 5 to 7 days.

Nothing tastes as good as sweet corn picked at the peak of ripeness
and plunged immediately into boiling water. To ensure a steady supply,
make a new sowing every 2 weeks until early summer.

Corn has been a crop in the Americas for thousands of years. When
Columbus arrived, it was being grown in five colors: black, white, red,
yellow, and blue. Its Native American name, *mahiz,* means "our life."

GARDEN HINT: Don't rush to plant your corn. Cold, wet soil makes
seeds more likely to rot than germinate. Corn is wind pollinated. When
you first see silk appear from the tips of small ears, harvest should
be just under 3 weeks away.

MARTHA'S SELECTION: 'Breeder's Bicolor' hybrid—A yellow-and-
white bicolor with sweet, tender kernels on 8-inch-long ears. Grows
to about 6 feet tall. Days to harvest: 73.

'BREEDER'S BICOLOR'
SWEET CORN

**'BRANDYWINE'
TOMATO**

TOMATO

Lycopersicon esculentum

SPACE OR THIN TO: FOR INDETERMINATE TOMATOES, SPACE EVERY 24 INCHES IN ROWS 30 INCHES APART IF ON TRELLISES; EVERY 30 INCHES IN ROWS 36 INCHES APART IF SPRAWLING. FOR DETERMINATE TOMATOES, PLANT EVERY 30 INCHES IN ROWS 30 INCHES APART; **SUN:** FULL; **SOIL:** RICH, FERTILE, WELL DRAINED

SOW: Indoors 4 to 6 weeks before the last frost; move as often as twice to larger pots to avoid root crowding, ending up in 4-inch pots. Transplant 1 week after last frost. Sow seeds ¼ inch deep. Germinates in 7 to 14 days at 70 to 80 degrees.

On seed packets and transplant labels, you'll find tomatoes described as "indeterminate" or "determinate." Indeterminate cultivars continue to grow throughout the warm weather, bearing fruit in a gradual stream, an ideal situation for those who want just a fruit or two at a time for a salad or sandwich. Determinate cultivars stop growing when they mature, and bear the bulk of their fruits in a single flood—a pattern that is more convenient for sauce-makers and home canners.

GARDEN HINT: Rotate plantings to avoid perpetuating soil-borne diseases; don't plant tomatoes, or their relatives the peppers, potatoes, and eggplants, in a spot where these plants have grown in the past 3 to 4 years. For a stronger, healthier plant, bury a lanky tomato transplant horizontally in a trench with just the tip and a couple of sets of leaves exposed—roots will grow along the buried stem. Let the ground warm, and give the plants a chance to establish themselves before mulching, which will let the soil retain moisture and control weeds. Too much heat—days above

(Tomato *continued*)

95 degrees or nights above 75 degrees—kills the pollen and prevents flowers from setting fruit. Tomatoes will start producing again when temperatures drop.

MARTHA'S SELECTIONS: 'Brandywine'—One of the most popular and best-tasting heirlooms. Flavorful but not acidic, a large-lobed beefsteak-shaped tomato with a thin, pinkish-red skin. Very vigorous vine; best if staked, caged, or trellised. Indeterminate. Size of fruits: large, 10 to 16 ounces; days to harvest: 80. 'Sun Gold' hybrid—This bite-size cherry tomato has an intense orangish color and an exceptionally sweet taste. Disease and crack resistant; grows on vigorous, tall vines. Indeterminate. Size of fruits: up to 1 ounce, 1 inch across; days to harvest: 60. 'Green Zebra'—Striped green heirloom with low-acid, sweet-tangy flavor. Tall, vigorous plants should be caged, staked, or trellised. Indeterminate. Size of fruits: small, to 3 ounces; days to harvest: 80. 'Roma VF'—Sweet paste tomato with meaty flesh and few seeds. Compact plants with good disease resistance. Best grown in cages. Determinate. Size of fruits: pear or plum-shaped, 2 to 3 ounces; days to harvest: 75. 'Burpee's Supersteak' hybrid—Smooth-shouldered tomatoes with meaty flavor. High productivity and disease resistance in a very vigorous plant that does best on a trellis. Indeterminate. Size of fruits: 1 to 2 pounds; days to harvest: 80.

'BURPEE'S SUPERSTEAK'
HYBRID TOMATO

'SUN GOLD' HYBRID
TOMATO

'GREEN ZEBRA'
TOMATO

'ROMA VF'
TOMATO

'CRIMSON SWEET'
WATERMELON

WATERMELON

Citrullus vulgaris

SPACE OR THIN TO: 3 PLANTS PER HILL OR 30 INCHES APART; **SUN:** FULL; **SOIL:** RICH, LIGHT, WELL DRAINED

SOW: North of zone 8, sow this annual fruit indoors in peat pots, 3 to 4 weeks before transplanting (transplant 2 to 3 weeks after last frost). From zone 8 southward, direct sow 2 weeks after danger of frost is past. Sow seeds ½ inch deep; outdoors, sow 6 seeds per hill in hills 6 to 8 feet apart, or sow 1 seed every 2 feet in rows 6 feet apart. Germinates in 5 to 7 days. Days to harvest: 80-85.

This is an easy crop where summers are long and warm. In the North, give watermelons a head start by sowing the seeds indoors, and grow the plants in a sunny, warm spot—a gentle, south-facing slope that is sheltered from the wind is ideal.

Although watermelons are thought of as being as American as apple pie, they originated in Namibia, in Africa, where they have been cultivated for 4,000 years.

GARDEN HINTS: In cool areas, use a floating row cover to keep young plants warm. Remove the cover when flowers appear so insects can pollinate the plants. Ripe melons make a dull thud when struck; slight pressure at the base of the stem causes the ripe fruit to separate from the vine.

MARTHA'S SELECTION: 'Crimson Sweet'—An award-winning, vigorous, round watermelon with firm, dark-red flesh. Grows well in a variety of areas and is disease resistant. The beautiful shell is light green with dark-green stripes. Size: 20 to 30 pounds; days to harvest: 80 to 85.

'EARLY ACORN' HYBRID
WINTER SQUASH

WINTER SQUASH

Cucurbita moschata, C. pepo

SPACE OR THIN TO: 1 TO 2 PLANTS PER HILL; **SUN:** FULL;
SOIL: RICH, FERTILE, WELL DRAINED

SOW: Direct sow 2 to 3 weeks after the last frost. Indoors, start in individual peat pots 3 weeks before transplanting outdoors. Transplant after all danger of frost is past and the soil has warmed. Sow seeds 1 inch deep, 5 or 6 seeds per hill, in hills placed every 3 feet in rows 8 feet apart. Germinates in 7 to 10 days.

Surprisingly, perhaps, winter squashes grow best in hot weather. They got their name because their fruits last so well when stored in a root cellar or cool pantry, and so were a staple of the winter diet.

GARDEN HINTS: Winter squash ripen in fall and should be allowed to mature fully on the vine. Don't harvest them until frost withers the leaves and they have developed the hard skin they need for long storage. Plants make a great ground cover on a sunny slope.

MARTHA'S SELECTIONS: *C. pepo* 'Early Acorn' hybrid—Sweeter and drier than other acorn squashes. Yields about 5 fruits per plant. Stores well at 45 to 50 degrees without curing. Size: 6 inches or more; days to harvest: 95 to 105. *C. moschata* 'Waltham Butternut'—Light tan with rich, flavorful, orange flesh. Keeps for 6 months at 45 to 50 degrees. Size: 9 to 10 inches; days to harvest: 75.

'WALTHAM BUTTERNUT'
WINTER SQUASH

INDEX